Phil Maggitti

Pugs

Everything About Purchase, Care, Nutrition, Behavior, and Training

BARRON'S

CONTENTS

LONG STORY SHORT: THE PUG DOG'S HISTORY

Like all other dogs, the Pug ultimately descended from the wolf, a special variety of lap wolf, no doubt, that was waited on hand and paw by the other wolves.

Although we cannot know for certain, most authorities believe the Pug is an Oriental breed, whose common ancestors are the Pekingese and the lion dog—the ancestor of today's Shih Tzu—and whose country of origin is China.

Estimates of the time at which the Pug originated are varied. Prior to 400 B.C.E., some observers say; in 600 B.C.E., others say; more than 1,800 years ago, say others still. Much of this uncertainty can be blamed on the Emperor Chin Shih, who destroyed all records, scrolls, and art relating to the Pug sometime during his dynasty, which lasted from 255 to 205 B.C.E.

From Munchkin to Monkey

The first recorded appearance of *pug* in the English language occurred in 1566. Pug was a term of endearment then—the equivalent of "little munchkin." Although pug was applied to persons but rarely to animals at first, by 1600 pug had acquired two additional meanings—"courtesan" and "bargeman"—and by 1664 pug also meant "demon," "imp," "sprite," "monkey," and "ape."

Not until the middle of the next century did *The Oxford English Dictionary* (OED) define pug as "a dwarf breed of dog resembling a bull-dog in miniature." The OED also added that the Pug "on account of its affectionate nature [was] much kept as a pet."

Some people believe the word *pug* was applied to monkeys at first, but after certain facial resemblances between monkeys and the little dogs with the curly tails had been noted, pug was applied to those dogs too. This application was noted as early as 1731 in England. Persons subscribing to this theory point out

Name Games

As other Pug lovers would do in later centuries, the Chinese had several names for Pugs, including *Foo* or *Fu* dog, Lo-Chiang-Sze, Lo-Chiang, Pia dog, and Hand dog.

that pugs were called *pug dogs* originally to distinguish them from pug monkeys.

Other people wrote that pug was derived from the Latin *pugnus*, meaning fist, because the pug's profile resembled a clenched fist. Still others believe pug is a corruption of Puck, the name of the mischievous fairy in Shakespeare's *A Midsummer Night's Dream*. The puckish nature of the Pug seems to support this theory, but the OED does not. After acknowledging that pug "agrees completely in sense with Puck," the OED cautions that pug "is not easily accounted for as a mere phoenetic variant" of Puck.

Like so many questions regarding animal history, inquiries about the origin of the Pug's name cannot be answered with certainty. Our money is on the borrowed-from-the-monkey-name theory; but before we leave this question, we should point out that pug also has been applied to lambs, hares, squirrels, ferrets, salmon, moths, small locomotives, fox, trout, clay, and the footprints of any beast.

Dutch Treat

Although no one knows for certain when or where the Pug arrived in Europe, the Dutch usually get credit for its importation. Called the Mopshond, the Dutch word for "grumble," the Pug was greatly favored as a lap warmer by Dutch ladies, who tried to avoid freezing in their large, unheated houses by placing a Pug or two on their laps.

The Dutch also are credited with introducing the Pug to England. This event is supposed to have occurred in November 1688 when the Dutch prince William III of Orange and his wife, the English princess Mary, landed at Torbay in South Devonshire to ascend the English throne. According to virtually all Pug historians and authors, by the time William III and his Pugs arrived in England, the Pug had been anointed the official dog of the House of Orange in the Netherlands.

The Pug owed this status to the heroics of a dog named Pompey, who had saved the life of William III's grandfather, Prince William the Silent. The governor of Holland and a fancier of Pugs, William the Silent left the Netherlands for Germany in 1567 after Philip II of Spain had sent an army to Holland to put down an armed revolt that had arisen the year before.

Unwilling to remain silent forever, William led a counteroffensive against the Spanish army in 1572. One night during that campaign, as William lay sleeping in his tent at Hermigny, assassins came creeping. Pompey began to bark in an effort to warn his master. Finally he jumped on William's face to alert him. Consequently, wrote Sir Roger Williams in 1618, "untill the Prince's dying day [1584], he kept one of that dog's race; so did many of his friends and followers."

"That dog's race" was described by Williams as "a white little hounde," but most observers concluded, as did Susan Graham Weall, author of *The Pug*, that "it can reasonably be thought, from other parts of its description, that it actually was an ancestor of the modern Pug."

The other part of the little white hounde's description that seems to have convinced Weall and others that Pompey was a Pug was Sir Roger's report that Pompey and others of his "race" had crooked noses called "camuses." That, we are told, clinches the argument because camus is a French word meaning "flat-nosed" or "pug-nosed." Moreover, the likeness of a Pug dog lies at the feet of William I's effigy in Holland's Delft Cathedral.

The Loyal Opposition

Traditional claims about the Pug's role in Dutch history have been challenged by Robert Hutchinson, the author of *For the Love of Pugs*. "At first blush," writes Hutchinson "the cumulative effect of this mass of circumstantial evidence would seem to confirm beyond a reasonable doubt the argument for the Pug" being a great favorite in the House of Orange and the savior of William the Silent.

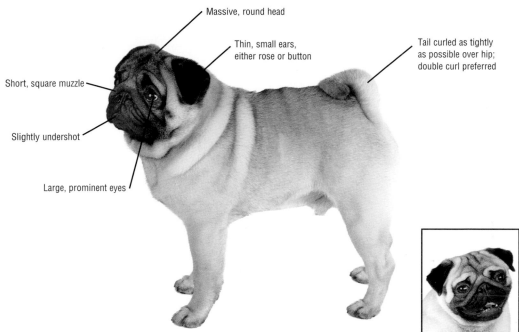

Massive, round head

Thin, small ears,
either rose or button

Tail curled as tightly
as possible over hip;
double curl preferred

Short, square muzzle

Slightly undershot

Large, prominent eyes

Breed standard
Part blueprint and part wish list, the Pug breed standard describes the ideal Pug.

Nevertheless, continues Hutchinson, closer inspection "discloses a house of cards" in the House of Orange accounts.

The first joker in the deck is the effigy of William I in the Delft Cathedral. Citing personal reports from several Dutch dog fanciers, Hutchinson argues that the dog at William's feet in the cathedral is a Kooikerhondje. This small, white hound with bright orange markings is little known outside Holland; but inside Holland the Kooikerhondje, not the Pug, is "universally credited" with saving William I. Insiders also report that the Kooiker was the mascot of the House of Orange. In further support of this claim, Hutchinson cites additional popular and some scholarly evidence.

In a Dutch-made television biography of William I, a Kooiker was cast in the role of William's canine savior; and in *Nederlandse historien,* first published in 1642, the Dutch historian Pieter Corneliszoon Hooft credits a Kooikerhondje named Kuntze with saving William's life.

Hutchinson also points out that the English word *camus* meant something different in Sir Roger Williams' time than the French word *camus* does today. The latter is, in fact, a synonym for "pug-nosed," but that meaning did not come into existence until the nineteenth century. In Sir Roger Williams' (and Prince William's) time the English word *camus* described a nose that curved upward

Pugs in Black

Black Pugs, at least one researcher believes, were developed in Japan in the late ninth or early tenth centuries. From there the black Pugs' appearance in other parts of the world shadowed that of their fawn relatives. Some of the earliest black Pugs—and some of the earliest fawn Pugs as well—were decorated with patches of white in their coats.

or downward, not a nose that was marching toward the back of its owner's skull.

In his measured argument Hutchinson further asserts that there is "no documentary evidence from the seventeenth century to indicate that the Pug was an Orange mascot." Furthermore "Dutch art of the seventeenth century reveals no images of Pugs at all." Finally "there appears to be no hard contemporary evidence of the presence of Pugs in England prior to 1730." (The careful reader will recall that the first instance of the word pug being used to describe a dog was not noted until 1731 in England.)

Continental Favorites

The Pug's popularity was not confined to England and Holland. He had friends in high places throughout the rest of Europe, too. One of the Pug's greatest champions was Josephine Bonaparte, wife of the emperor Napoleon. Josephine's Pug, Fortune, bit Napoleon on the leg when he was climbing into bed on his and Josephine's wedding night in 1796. Fortune survived that encounter, but he did not survive a challenge to the cook's English Bulldog. Following this reversal of fortune, Fortune was replaced by another Pug, also named Fortune. When the unfortunate Josephine was imprisoned at Les Carmes, Napoleon sent love notes to her hidden in Fortune II's collar.

The Pug also was well known in Italy and Spain during the eighteenth century. In 1789 a Mrs. Piozzi wrote in her journal, "The little pug dog or Dutch mastiff has quitted London for Padua, I perceive. Every carriage I meet here has a pug in it."

A painting by Goya places the Pug in Spain, where it was known as the *Dogullo*, by 1785; and the use of the word *Mopsorden* (Order of the Pug) by Masons in Germany, who were excommunicated by the Pope in 1736, serves to date the Pug in that country.

The Pug in America

The first Pugs imported to the United States arrived shortly after the Civil War had ended. The breed was one of 15 recognized by the American Kennel Club (AKC), which was founded in 1884; but after a promising start in this country, Pugs were overshadowed by longer-coated toy breeds such as the Pekingese and Pomeranian. From 1900 to 1920 few people bred Pugs, and many shows drew no Pug entry at all. In 1915 the AKC registered only 32 Pugs, and in 1920 that number dropped to five. At that point the Pug ranked 51st out of 58 breeds then recognized by the AKC.

The first Pug dog club in this country was started in 1931, but that club did not last much past its first show, which was held in 1937. In the early 1950s the Pug Dog Club of America, the parent club of the breed, was founded. Whether by coincidence or calculation the Pug enjoyed its first popularity surge during the fifties. Indeed the Pug more than quintupled its annual registrations with the AKC between 1950 and 1960, soaring from 958 new registrations—and 31st place on the AKC hit parade—to 5,080 registrations, and 17th place out of 106 breeds.

The Pug suffered a setback during the next two decades, and by 1980 had slipped to 40th on the AKC list. Pugs have pulled themselves up by their registration slips in the meantime, and in 2008 the breed ranked 15th out of 156 breeds then registered by the AKC.

A PUG OF YOUR OWN

If you have decided that your life would be greatly improved with a Pug in it, congratulations, you are a person of fine taste and sound character. Now all you have to do is locate a person of fine taste and sound character with a Pug for sale.

Unfortunately there are no screening tests required of persons who breed and sell dogs. The phone number you dial to inquire about puppies may connect you with a conscientious individual motivated solely by the love of the breed, or you may find yourself talking to someone who would sell a puppy to a band of devil worshipers as long as they paid with a certified check or postal money order.

Where to Find a Pug

Breeders may advertise in dog magazines, in the classified sections of newspapers, on bulletin boards in veterinary offices, in grooming shops, feed stores, on the Internet, and in *Pug Talk*, a publication no Pug lover should be without. Pug breeders also may be found at dog shows, which are advertised in newspapers and dog magazines, in veterinarians' offices, and on the Internet (just search for "dog shows").

A breeder's contribution to a Pug's development can scarcely be overrated. Even though temperament and good health are inherited to some extent, the way a puppy is raised is at least equally important in shaping his personality and in determining his state of health. Puppies that are not handled frequently between the ages of three and 14 weeks are less likely to develop into well-adjusted adults than are puppies that receive abundant handling and attention during this time.

A breeder who produces more than three or four litters a year, or who was raising two or three other litters while your puppy's litter was maturing, may not have had time to socialize every puppy in those litters properly. A breeder who raises only two or three litters a year—and preferably not at the same time—has more opportunity to give each of those puppies the individual attention he deserves.

Pet shops do not breed the puppies they sell; nevertheless pet shops ought to provide the names, addresses, and phone numbers of the persons who do. If you are interested in a pet-shop Pug and that information is not available, proceed with caution because you are proceeding with less information about the puppy than you would have if you were buying directly from his breeder.

If the pet shop provides the name and address of a puppy's breeder, and if that person lives nearby, call to arrange a visit so that you might observe the conditions in which the puppy was raised. If the breeder lives far away, telephone or e-mail to ask any questions you might have about the puppy.

In addition, you should call the humane association or Better Business Bureau nearest to the place where the breeder lives to ask if the breeder enjoys a good reputation in that area. Matter of fact, you should make that inquiry no matter where you buy a puppy.

Note: Recommending this sort of caution does not imply that buying from a pet shop is more risky than buying from a breeder. What is implied is that the buyer should find out as much as possible about a Pug's background before deciding whether or not to buy that Pug.

Animal shelters sometimes offer Pugs for adoption. If you are willing to wait for a Pug until one is surrendered at a shelter, ask to be put on the shelter's waiting list.

Breed rescue clubs exist to find homes for Pugs that have been given up for adoption. Members of rescue clubs often cooperate with animal shelters by providing foster homes for lost, abandoned, or surrendered Pugs, feeding and caring for them while trying to locate suitable new owners. Animal shelters in your area may be able to provide the name of a Pug rescue organization. If not, the Internet will be able to help.

Questions to Ask Yourself

1. Male or Female? Some dog owners, because of inclination or experience, prefer the company of one sex over another. Pugs, however, do not make such distinctions; and all Pugs will make fine companions if they are given love, a supply of things to chew, and a place on or near your bed at night.

2. Puppy, Adolescent, or Adult? If Pug puppies were more appealing, they would be illegal. What they lack in brainpower they make up for in curiosity. What they lack in experience they make up for in exuberance. They stomp joyfully through their food bowls and their days, tails wagging, heads lolling, eyes shining, bellies and hearts overflowing.

The adolescent Pug, while not quite so busy as all that, is just as appealing. The adult Pug, too, remains young at heart; and just as the

adolescent Pug is not much different from a puppy, an adult is not much different from an adolescent. Indeed it is difficult to determine where adolescence leaves off and adulthood begins with Pugs. Even elderly Pugs—who may not play with the same determination that younger dogs exhibit—retain their enthusiasm for the finer things in life such as marrow bones, leisurely walks, and car rides.

3. Fawn or Black? A Pug's physical characteristics are governed by genes, which transmit instructions regarding the development of physical characteristics from an individual to his or her offspring. Genes are arranged in pairs on chromosomes. Because the gene for black is dominant over the gene for fawn, a Pug will be black if he inherits one black gene and one fawn gene—or two black genes—from his parents. He will be fawn only if he inherits

two fawn genes. As there is only one or two genes' worth of difference between a black and a fawn Pug, the choice of color is a matter of personal preference.

4. One Dog or Two? If you are acquiring your first puppy, consider getting two, even if there is someone at home during the day and your puppy will not have to spend much time alone. A puppy needs the company of another dog that will be interested in playing long after humans have been worn out.

If you already have a dog—preferably one that is five years old or younger—it is not too late to get a second dog. Before you do, consider this: two dogs are not as easy to keep, feed, clean, and look after as one; nor, in some cases, will you simply be doubling your work load by adding a second Pug. Whether your dog-related chores increase by a factor of three or four, however, the pleasure that two dogs provide is always more than twice as great as the pleasure that one can give you. If buying a second Pug would tax your budget, adopt a dog from a local shelter, a dog that is roughly the same age and will grow up to be roughly the same size as the Pug you are purchasing.

5. Show Dog or Pet? Unless you are planning to show and/or breed your Pug, you want a pet-quality dog. "Pet quality" describes a dog with some cosmetic "flaw" that argues against his breeding or showing success. Pet-quality Pugs may have narrow muzzles, large noses, tails that are not as tightly curled as a show dog's, or some other "fault." None of these surface features in any way detracts from the Pug's sterling personality, for every Pug is a quality dog at heart.

How Much Is That Doggie?

The price of a Pug is determined by age, quality, supply, demand, and geography. Young Pugs, roughly ten to twelve weeks old or so, are generally priced between $500 and $900 if they are not considered suitable for breeding and showing. These "pet-quality" Pugs will make lovely companions if they are healthy and have been socialized properly.

The Age of Consent

Puppyhood is one of the special joys of dog owning. Dogs are dogs their entire lives, but they are puppies for only a few precious months. Thus new owners are eager to take their puppies home as soon as possible, but responsible breeders do not let puppies go until they are between ten and twelve weeks old. By that age a puppy has been weaned properly, has

CHECKLIST

The Healthy Puppy Checklist

You do not have to be a veterinarian to recognize basic signs of good health or sickness. A puppy's health is reflected in the way he looks.

	Positive signs	Problem signs
✔ eyes	shiny, bright, clear	dull, teary, bloodshot, caked
✔ nose	cool, slightly damp	warm, dry, caked
✔ gums	pink	pale, inflamed
✔ ears	clean	wax, dirt, ear mite debris
✔ body	soft, perhaps a bit plump	emaciated or pot-bellied
✔ coat	clean and smooth	bald patches, scabs, flea dirt
✔ tail area	clean, dry	wet or crusty with dried diarrhea

- A puppy with teary eyes may be in poor health, especially if his nose is dry or if it feels warm. Inflamed gums may indicate gingivitis; a puppy with pale gums may be anemic. Wax inside a puppy's ears may simply be a sign of neglect, but if his ears are caked with dirt, the puppy may have ear mites.
- If a puppy's ribs are sticking out or if he is pot-bellied, he may be undernourished, or he may have worms. A puppy with a dull-looking coat or one dotted with scabs, tiny specks of dirt, or bald spots may have ringworm or fleas.
- A puppy with wet hindquarters may develop urine scalding; if they are dirty, he may have diarrhea. Both urine scalding and diarrhea are signs of potential poor health.

been eating solid food for several weeks, and has begun to make the transition to adulthood.

Puppies younger than ten weeks are still babies. Take them away from their mothers and their siblings at that age, and the stress of adjusting to new surroundings may cause some puppies to become sick, to be difficult to housetrain, or to nurse on blankets or sofa cushions, a habit they sometimes keep the rest of their lives. No matter how tempting a seven-week-old puppy might be, he will adjust better if he is allowed to remain in his original home until he is several weeks older.

The Pug Personality Scale

Any puppy that comes racing over to check you out as soon as he sees you will probably make a fine companion. So will the puppy that responds to your wiggling a few fingers or dragging a small toy along the floor about 6 inches (15 cm) in front of him.

Well-adjusted, healthy puppies are curious about fingers, toys, and anything else that moves within sight. Nervous or timid puppies, or those that are not feeling well, are more cautious. Poorly adjusted puppies head for cover.

If you have other pets or children at home, the inquisitive, in-your-face puppy is the best choice. The bashful puppy might make a fine companion, too, but he may take longer to adjust, and is, perhaps, better left for experienced dog owners who currently are without pets or young children.

As for the little one behind the chair: shy puppies need love too, plenty of it. If you have no other pets or if you plan to acquire two puppies at once and have the time and

patience required to nurture such a reluctant puppy, you should spare a thought for this little guy.

Contracts and Papers

Breeders should provide sales contracts when selling puppies. Most contracts specify the price of the puppy, the amount of the deposit required to hold the puppy, if any, when the balance of the payment is due, and so on.

Most contracts allow the puppy buyer three to five working days after receiving a puppy to take him to a veterinarian for an examination. If the veterinarian discovers any preexisting conditions such as luxating patella or a heart murmur, the buyer should have the right to return the puppy at the seller's expense and to have the purchase price refunded.

Deposit

When buyers give a breeder a deposit on a puppy, they should write "deposit for thus-

and-such puppy" on the memo line of the check. Buyers should make a similar notation when writing a check for the balance of the payment. Sellers should provide receipts for all payments. They should specify in advance—and preferably in writing—whether a deposit is refundable if the buyer decides not to take the puppy. Buyers also should remember that once a breeder has accepted money or some other consideration in return for reserving a puppy, the breeder and the buyer have entered into an option contract. The breeder cannot legally revoke or renegotiate the offer if he or she decides to keep the puppy.

Read a contract thoroughly before signing it. Contracts are legally binding after they have been signed by both parties. If a contract contains any stipulations you do not understand or do not wish to agree to, discuss these issues with the breeder before signing.

In addition to their dog's pedigree, new owners usually receive a registration slip that they can fill out and send, along with the appropriate fee, to the administrative office of the American Kennel Club or to another association if that is where the puppy is eligible to be registered. The association then returns a certificate of ownership to the new owner(s).

Persons buying a dog or puppy that has been registered already by his breeder will receive an owner's certificate. There is a transfer-of-ownership section on the back of the certificate that must be signed by the breeder and the new owner. Once the required signatures are present, the new owner mails the certificate, with the appropriate transfer fee, to the

organization in which the dog or puppy was registered. That organization will send back a new, amended certificate of ownership to the new owner(s).

Health Certificates

Health certificates, along with vaccination and deworming records, are the most important documents that accompany a puppy to his new home. Do not accept a puppy without these papers, and be sure the health certificate you receive with your puppy was issued by a veterinarian within ten days of the time you receive your puppy.

Some breeders, especially those who produce a large volume of puppies, save money by giving vaccinations themselves. There is nothing illegal about this practice, yet there is more to immunizing a puppy than drawing vaccine into a syringe and pushing the plunger. Few, if any, breeders are capable of examining puppies as thoroughly as a veterinarian can before administering vaccinations. This examination is important because vaccine given to a sick puppy will do more harm than good. Thus a puppy should be seen by a veterinarian at least once before he is sold, preferably before his first vaccination.

Why You Should Alter Your Pug

There are compelling medical reasons for altering (either spaying or neutering) your Pug. Spaying a female is accomplished through a procedure known as an ovariohysterectomy, during which the uterus and ovaries are removed surgically under general anesthesia. Spaying eliminates the possibility that a female will develop uterine cancer later in life, and according to the American College of Veterinary Surgeons, spaying "vastly" reduces the chance that a female will develop breast cancer. Indeed if a female is spayed before she goes into season (or heat) for the first time, she is "200 times less likely" to develop cancer of the mammary glands. Neutering (or castrating) a male greatly reduces his risk of contracting testicular and/or prostate cancers.

Altering a dog also confers benefits on you because altered dogs make more civilized companions. Unneutered males are wont to lift their legs to anoint vertical objects with urine as a means of marking territory and attracting females. Unneutered males also are inclined to make sexual advances at your guests' legs and to regard any other dog as a potential mate or sparring partner.

Unspayed females, for their part, generally come into season twice a year. This condition is accompanied by a swelling of the vulva, blood-stained rugs, and the occasional visit from a neighborhood dog that pees all over your doorstep. A heat lasts 21 days, on average, and they will be among the longest 21 days you ever endure.

There are socially responsible reasons for altering your Pug, too. With tens of thousands

TIP

Payment Due

The cost of altering a dog varies according to geography and veterinarians' price structures. Some veterinarians charge as little as $50 for the procedure; others may charge more than $300. Humane societies, animal shelters, and low-cost spay-and-neuter clinics charge, on average, between $45 and $135, depending on the weight of the dog. The cost of spaying a female, because it is more complicated, ranges from $50 to $175. The American Society for the Prevention of Cruelty to Animals maintains a free and low-cost spay/neuter database at *www.aspca.org/pet-care/spayneuter*.

of puppies born each day, the decision to bring more puppies into the world is not one to be made lightly. For all but a few people it is not one that should be made at all. The pet over-population problem cannot be solved by the unrestricted breeding of puppies. The millions of healthy dogs killed in shelters each year for want of good homes argue for restraint and common sense on the part of humans, especially those who call themselves animal lovers.

When to Alter Your Pug

Most veterinarians recommend that females be spayed when they are about six months old and that males be neutered when they are seven to ten months old. At these ages sexual development is nearly complete, but undesirable traits have not become habits.

OFF TO A FLYING START

Bringing a new Pug home is not a spur-of-the-moment idea, like deciding to have some friends over to watch a movie. You cannot simply gather up the mess that has accumulated since the last time people came by and stuff it into a closet, then dash to the convenience store for snacks and beer.

While you are counting the days until your new Pug's arrival, spare a thought for his comfort, safety, and amusement. That thought will lead you to planning menus, doing some serious shopping, placing the knickknacks to best advantage, and really putting on the dog.

The Pug Puppy's Wish List

Shopping for supplies is one of the joys of being a new Pug owner. That joy is compounded by the variety of merchandise available to the person who wishes to provide her new Pug with the trappings of the good life. Never has so much been available so readily from so many sources—pet shops, dog-show vendors, pet-supply warehouses, and websites. The possibilities are limited only by your determination and your credit card balance.

✔ **Food and water bowls:** metal or ceramic are best, as long as the ceramic bowl does not contain lead, which can be poisonous to dogs. Plastic or rubber bowls can retain odors even when washed thoroughly. They may also cause skin allergies around your Pug's mouth and chin.

✔ **Rubber guards:** place on the bottom of food and water bowls to keep them from sliding and, perhaps, spilling their contents.

✔ **Place mats:** decorator vinyl or plain rubber to protect your carpet or floor.

✔ **Collar:** available in leather or nylon, with buckle or snap fasteners. Most leather collars have belt-buckle fasteners; most nylon collars have the plastic, click-together kind. Nylon web collars with click-together fasteners are the choice for a young Pug puppy. They are inexpensive to replace when outgrown, easier and faster to put on and to remove, and because they do not shrink or dry stiff after being wet, they can be washed when they become dirty.

✔ **Harness:** does not put pressure on a dog's windpipe if he lunges forward as you are walking him, and there is no danger of his slipping out of it.

✔ **Leash:** available in leather, cotton, or nylon, fixed length or retractable. A retractable leash allows you to keep your Pug nearby when necessary or to permit him more freedom in open spaces.

✔ **Toys:** dogs are seldom happier than when they are chewing on something: a stuffed toy, rubber ball, or some other safe, sturdy plaything. Before buying any toy for your Pug, imagine how it might cause him harm. If there is any chance that it could, do not buy it. Any toy with a bell or whistle on the inside or a button or cute little tail on the outside should be avoided.

✔ **First aid kit:** see page 58, for a full description of its contents.

✔ **Crate:** provides your Pug with a secure den; provides you with a feeling of security when you cannot supervise your Pug. Whether you choose a heavy-duty plastic travel kennel or a wire crate with a removable floor pan, a crate should be small enough so that your Pug will feel cozy in it, but large enough to accommodate him when he is full grown. A crate that measures 24 inches (61 cm) long, 21 inches (53 cm) high, and 19 inches (48 cm) wide meets those requirements. The bottom of the crate should be covered with a soft mat equipped with a washable cover.

✔ **Food:** feed your Pug a premium, all-natural, holistic dog food, preferably made from organic, human-grade ingredients. The first ingredient of a superior dog food is meat; the second and third ingredients should be meat or meat meal. Avoid foods that contain corn, cornmeal, and/or wheat, as some dogs are allergic to them. Any grains in your Pug's food should be in whole form so that they supply more fiber, vitamins, and minerals; grains should compose no more than 10 percent of his diet.

✔ **Grooming tools:** a brush, comb, de-shedding tool, nail clipper, styptic powder, Q-tips, shampoo, and a flea-removal tool. Page 34 explains how to use these implements.

✔ **Dog beds:** available in many sizes, colors, materials, and designs. Some are round, some oval; some are made of Thinsulate, some are made of medical-grade polyfoam, some are made like bean bags, and some even are heated. Whatever its construction and design, a dog bed should have a removable, washable cover. Beds provide insulation, support, and comfort for your Pug. They also provide you with a means of containing the hair your Pug sheds.

✔ **Baby gate:** after your Pug has been house-trained, there may be times when you will want to confine him to a room in which you are not present. A sturdy, hinged, swing-open baby gate is essential for those times.

Pug-proofing Your House

Pugs are built for comfort, not speed. They should be able to jump onto a sofa or a bed easily enough, but they are not great leapers; and they are, for the most part, not so tall that they can stand on their hind legs and seize food off the kitchen table. Thus, Pug-proofing your house consists mainly of keeping objects that you do not want chewed at a height where your Pug cannot reach them.

• If there are any rooms you do not want your Pug to investigate, keep the doors to those rooms closed. If there are fragile objects in the rooms your Pug is allowed to visit, put them out of reach.

- Mark sliding glass doors in some fashion so that your Pug does not go charging into them.
- Make sure all electrical cords are intact. If your dog or puppy begins chewing on electrical cords, wrap them in heavy tape or cover them with plastic conduit, which you can buy in an auto-supply shop. Until you are certain your Pug has not developed a taste for electrical cords, unplug all appliances that are not in use, if necessary. To keep your Pug from getting a charge out of electrical sockets, cover them with plastic, plug-in socket guards, which you can buy at a hardware store.
- Keep all kitchen and bathroom cleansers, chemicals, cleaners, and toilet articles in cabinets that can be closed or locked securely.
- Keep the lids on all trash receptacles tightly closed. Consider replacing trash containers whose swing-open lids could be dislodged if your Pug overturns the containers.
- Put sewing supplies and yarn away when you are finished using them.
- Do not leave rubber bands, hot irons, cigarettes, plastic bags, or pieces of string or yarn lying around.

In short, you must learn to think like a Pug. Look for any potential accident—tinsel on a Christmas tree or a dangling tablecloth—waiting for a Pug to make it happen.

Welcoming the Newcomer

You have bought every item on your shopping list and a few extra items as well. You have set up the crate and dog bed. You have made a final safety check of the house. Now it is time to bring your new Pug home.

If you are unfortunate enough to have to work during the week, schedule the homecom-

ing for the start of a weekend or vacation. Remember that even though you have planned carefully for this day, it will come as a major surprise to a puppy, who will be leaving his mother, playmates, people, and the only home he has ever known.

Most puppies adjust swimmingly. They enter their new homes with wiggly excitement and great curiosity. Other puppies—and some older dogs—may not be so self-assured. Do not be surprised if your newcomer looks apprehensive. Keep the welcoming party to a minimum, and reassure your new friend by petting him and speaking to him gently. After he has taken the measure of your household, he will become more at ease, but that process should be taken one room and one or two family members at a time.

Your Pug will feel more comfortable in his new home if he has something from his former home on hand: a favorite toy, a blanket or bed, or a favorite food. These items give off familiar, comforting smells that are reassuring in a strange, new world.

Crate Training

You should introduce your new Pug to his crate the first day you bring him home. After you have socialized with him for a while and have given him a chance to eliminate outdoors, place him in his crate with an interesting toy or treat. Leave the door open and stay in the room.

After your Pug is used to sitting in his crate with the door open, latch the door the next time you crate him. Stay in the room for a minute or two tidying up or going about some normal activity, then let him out of the crate and tell him what a good dog he is. If he barks, whines, or moans, ignore him, and do not let him out of the crate until he has been quiet for at least 30 seconds.

When your Pug is used to the idea of staying in his crate with the door closed, put him into the crate and leave the room for a minute, then return to the room and let him out of the crate, telling him what a good dog he is. Your Pug will learn to be relaxed about your comings and goings if you treat them matter-of-factly yourself, starting with the crate-training process.

As you teach your Pug to stay in his crate for longer periods, you are preparing him to use it as his bed and safe haven, his own private wolf den. A dog will not soil his bed unless he is nervous or in dire straits. Therefore, creating positive associations toward the crate will enable you to use it as an aid to house-training and as a secure place for your Pug when you cannot supervise him.

For the first few days after you bring your new Pug home, however, you should keep him near you, even if this means placing the crate in one part of the house during the day and moving it to your bedroom at night. This will do much to ease your Pug's adjustment to his new home.

Housetraining Without Tears

Housetraining consists of knowing that your dog has to relieve himself before he knows it. Fortunately this is almost as easy as it sounds. If you understand a puppy's behavior patterns, he can be housetrained with minimal difficulty.

Schedule

If your Pug is not housetrained when you get him, you will have to take him outdoors several times a day to the place where you want him to eliminate. The first trip out should occur immediately after the puppy wakes up in the morning. Make sure he has urinated and defecated before you take him in for breakfast, and make sure you praise him effusively.

TIP

Crate Strategy

To encourage their Pugs' attachment to the crate, some owners feed them their first meal or two in it. A toy in the crate also helps to promote that attachment.

In addition to his morning constitutional, your Pug will need to go outside about 10 to 15 minutes after each meal, immediately after waking up from a nap or engaging in spirited play, and any time he has been awake for more than two hours since the last time he was outside. He also ought to be taken outside the last thing before going to bed for the night and whenever he begins sniffing the floor and pacing about in a preoccupied manner. All in all, this amounts to roughly eight trips a day. What is more, young puppies cannot defer elimination much longer than four hours, so you will need to take your Pug out at least once during the night until he is three or four months old.

Do not expect your puppy to urinate and defecate every time he goes out. He ought to do one or the other on most trips, however, so do not take him back inside until you have given him ten minutes to perform. If he draws a blank—or if your rapidly developing instinct tells you he owes you some urine or solid waste—take him back into the house, put him in his crate with a toy, and try again in about 30 to 45 minutes.

As your puppy matures, he will need to go outside less frequently. After he is six months old, he will be eating twice a day instead of three times, so that is one fewer trip, and he probably will not have to go out right after breakfast if he has gone out just before eating. Normally our adult Pugs go out at 6:30 A.M., about 11:00 in the morning, 4:30 in the afternoon, and following dinner, which is served around 5:00. They get one last trip outside just before bedtime.

Accidents

When accidents occur, there is no point in striking a dog, pushing his face into his waste, or putting him into his crate for punishment. These reactions do nothing to further housetraining. Scolding or striking your dog only teaches him that you are unreliable and sometimes frightening. Stuffing him into his crate will make him view it as a jail. These outcomes are counterproductive. The secret of housetraining—indeed of all dog training—is to elicit the desired behavior from your dog, not to beat it into him.

Next to an observant owner, the puppy's crate is the most valuable aid in housetraining. Because you have helped your puppy to learn that his crate is a secure place, he will enter it willingly and use it as his bed during those times of the day when you cannot be with him. After he has been in his crate for any length of time, you should take him outside in case he has to eliminate.

The Empty House

If no one is at home during the day, or if no one is available to walk your puppy when you are not at home, you should not acquire a Pug puppy younger than four months of age. A puppy's physical limits for controlling urination and defecation argue against it. Also, keep in mind that an empty house is a lonely place for a Pug puppy, a dog meant to spend his days as part of a family.

Introducing Other Pets and Children

Caution is in order when introducing a Pug to other pets. The chances of hostilities breaking out increase with the age—and length of service—of the cat(s) or dog(s) already in residence. If you have an eight-year-old pet that always has been an only child, you probably should not get a new dog or puppy. If your pet is four years old or younger, you should be able to introduce your new Pug if you manage the introduction carefully, and if you keep in mind how you would feel if a stranger suddenly was brought to your house for an indefinite stay without your prior approval.

Do not include other pets in the welcoming party when you bring your new Pug home. Confine them in another room. After you have hung out with your new Pug for a few hours or so, allow him to meet your dog. If you have more than one dog, make the introductions one at a time, on successive days if necessary.

The best way to introduce an older dog to a new one is to put the new dog in his crate before letting the old dog into the room. If the older dog sniffs at the puppy but shows no hostility, put a leash on the older dog and let the puppy out of his crate after a minute or two. The less tension there is between the two dogs, the less tension you will feel on the leash. If your older dog flattens his ears or goes into a karate stance, tug on the leash to keep him from reaching the puppy. Take the older dog out of the room, and try the introduction again the following day. If the introduction goes well, give each dog a treat—the older dog first, of course—to reinforce their civil behavior.

Cats

Before letting your cat in to meet the puppy, be sure the cat's claws are clipped. Place the puppy in his crate first, then let the two animals sniff at one another and exchange small talk. If your cat is leash-trained, put a leash on him when you bring him in to meet the puppy. If not, stay close to him and the puppy. Chances are, a puppy-cat introduction will not go as smoothly as a puppy-dog introduction, but this does not mean that your puppy and your cat will not be able to coexist peacefully.

Children

Children who are too young or immature to treat a Pug properly can pose a threat to his safety and to his sense of confidence. Children must be mature enough to understand that Pugs do not like to be disturbed when they are eating or sleeping, that there is a right way to hold a Pug, and that Pugs are not toys to be lugged around the house. This is why parents with toddlers should wait to buy a dog or a puppy until their children are at least four years old.

Before agreeing to sell a puppy or a dog, breeders often want to meet a buyer's children. Conversely, buyers with children might do best to seek breeders whose puppies have been raised with youngsters underfoot.

Children do not always understand that what is fun for them may be annoying, or even painful, for a dog

✔ Explain that they must be careful to watch where they walk and run when the dog is around. Explain, too, that dogs often are frightened by loud, unfamiliar sounds.

✔ Ask children to speak and to play quietly until the dog gets used to them.

✔ Caution them not to pick the dog up until *you* feel he is comfortable enough in his new surroundings not to be frightened by an impromptu ride.

✔ Teach children the proper way to hold a dog: one hand under his rib cage just behind his front legs, the other hand under his bottom, with the dog's face pointing away from theirs. Have them practice this while sitting down in case they drop the dog or he jumps from their arms.

Dogs can inspire a sense of responsibility in children, but children never should be forced to take care of animals, and even when a child is a cooperative caregiver, parents should monitor the dog's feeding schedule, trips outdoors, and general condition.

The Collar

Introduce your puppy to a collar by putting one around his neck just before you feed him. Remove the collar after he has eaten but before you take him outside for his post-meal walk. After a few days, put the collar on him at other times during the day. Leave it on for a little longer each time. You can make this gradual introduction to the collar any time after your puppy is 12 weeks old.

After a puppy has gotten used to wearing a collar (this should not take more than a few days) add his identification and license tags to the collar. Your Pug need not wear a collar in the house or when he is playing in the yard, but he should wear a collar whenever he leaves his property.

The Harness

Introducing a harness to your Pug is scarcely more complicated than introducing a collar. Spend a few minutes playing with or petting your Pug, then set the harness on his back. If he recoils in disapproval, pet him a few seconds, remove the harness gently, and try again tomorrow. If he does not seem to mind the harness, hook it up and be done with it. Be sure to give him a treat once the harness is in place. Do not give him a treat if he recoils from the harness. Reassurance is enough in that case.

After your Pug consents to wearing the harness, leave it on for five or ten minutes a day for several days, then begin taking him for a walk in his harness so that he forms a pleasant association with it.

Leash Training

Step 1: The first time you put a leash on your Pug, allow him to drag it around a few minutes and give him one or two treats during that time, then remove the leash. Repeat this routine for two or three days.

Step 2: After your Pug is comfortable with the leash, pick up one end and hold it. Do not try to lead him anywhere; simply hold the leash while he moves about, following him wherever he goes. Remove the leash after three or four minutes.

Step 3: Now you are ready to have your Pug follow where you lead. With your Pug on your left side, his leash in your left hand, and your left arm by your side, show him the treat you have in your right hand. Take a step or two forward. If your Pug steps forward, too, move a few additional steps.

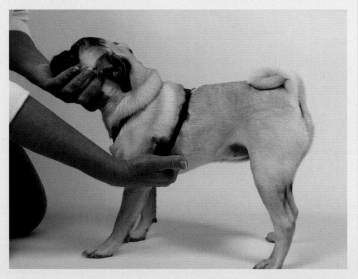

If he moves forward again, give him the treat. If he is reluctant to move, do not drag him. Show him the food again, this time holding it a little closer to his face. As soon as he moves toward it, say "*Good boy*," give him the food, and praise him for moving. If he refuses to move, pick him up, set him down a few paces forward, praise him for being a wonderful dog, but do not give him the treat. Then end the lesson for the day.

Your Pug should be willing to move a few steps the first day you have him on a leash. On subsequent days, increase the distance he must walk alongside you before he gets his treat.

Conduct leash training in your driveway or backyard. Do not try a public thoroughfare until your Pug walks attentively at your side.

Like any new lesson, leash-training should be taught with a good deal of patience in small steps. New experiences can be unsettling for any animal. The easier you make the lesson, the more likely your Pug is to grasp it readily. Remember that pleasing you is one of the most pleasing activities for your Pug. Do not let your training methods put speed bumps on his road to happiness.

ROUTINE CARE AND GROOMING

Grooming is the art of removing dead hair from your Pug so that he does not have to remove it himself. The more dead hair you remove from your Pug, the less you have to remove from the furniture, the rugs, and your clothing.

Although a Pug's coat looks short, Pugs *do* shed; and their hair has a life of its own, a half-life, actually, that has been reckoned at 4 million years!

The Right Tools

You will need all of the tools in the checklist on page 34 some of the time and some of the tools all of the time when you groom your Pug. Your selection will be driven by the nature of the grooming session—routine maintenance or a full makeover.

Grooming Technique

Pugs should be groomed on a table—an official store-bought kind or the kitchen table if no one is using it. Whatever your choice, put a rubber mat or a piece of carpet with nonslip backing on the table to give your Pug secure footing.

Always brush with the lie of the coat, the direction in which the coat grows. Do not push down on the brush constantly; glide it across your Pug's body smoothly with your wrist locked. You may need to brush with one hand while you steady the dog with the other. For example, place your free hand on your Pug's chest while you brush his back and sides; or place your free hand, palm up, on his belly while you brush his hindquarters or neck.

TIP

The Pug's Grooming Schedule

Pugs should be groomed twice a week. Because most Pugs enjoy being groomed, you should not have to coax your Pug to stand still during this procedure.

Brush (or comb) your Pug's legs downward, using short strokes. To groom a Pug's tail, hold it by the tip, unroll it gently, and brush softly with the lie of the coat.

Brushing not only keeps your Pug looking slick but also allows you to look for signs of trouble in his coat and skin. While you are brushing, check for flea dirt, skin rashes, or

bald spots. If you find flea dirt, treatment with a flea-killing product is in order (see page 50). Skin rashes or bald spots merit a visit to the

═■ TIP ■═

Brushing Up
The most useful brush for grooming a Pug is a pin brush with stainless steel bristles. If you want to be especially thorough about removing dead hair, use a slicker brush or a shedding blade occasionally.

═■ CHECKLIST ═

Grooming Tools
✔ brush(es)
✔ cotton swabs
✔ cotton balls
✔ nail clippers
✔ toothbrush and canine toothpaste
✔ lukewarm water
✔ Vaseline
✔ mineral oil or hydrogen peroxide
✔ paper cup or other receptacle for dead hair

veterinarian, who can assess the problem and prescribe treatment.

Tough as Nails

Your Pug's nails must be clipped regularly to prevent him from scratching himself or others while he plays. An additional reason for keeping his nails short is the fact that dogs walk on their toes as horses do, not on the soles of their feet as bears and humans prefer. If your Pug's nails are allowed to remain too long, he will rock back on his paws when he walks, putting a strain on his legs and interfering with his gait.

Many dogs, Pugs included, prefer that we keep our paws off theirs—a preference that can present problems when we try to clip their nails. If your Pug is not cool with this idea by the time he comes to live with you, you will have to get him used to it. Begin his rehabilitation by holding his paws casually or stroking them gently for a few seconds when you are petting him or watching television together. Continue this ritual until your handling his paws is no big deal to him.

Nail clipping, like death and rising tax rates, is unavoidable. Treats and lavish praise will make the ritual more pleasant; so will a friend or family member willing to hold your Pug while you clip.

Ear Care

A Pug's ears are not difficult to keep clean. A few cotton swabs or cotton balls and some mineral oil or hydrogen peroxide in a small container are the only materials you need. Dip the cotton swabs or cotton balls into the oil or peroxide (the choice is yours) and swab the visible parts of the ear carefully. Do not

plunge the cotton swab or cotton ball into the ear canal any farther than the eye can see, or you might do some damage. If you wish to

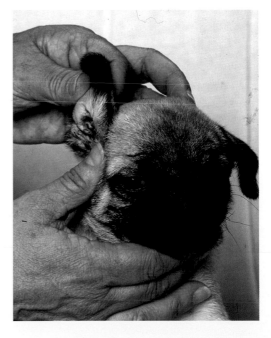

him if they are not kept clean. Once a week, or sooner if your Pug's face begins smelling like a clam bog, clean his wrinkles like so: hold his head gently in one hand and, with a Q-tip that has been dipped in warm water, clean any dirt or caked tears from his nose wrinkle. Be gentle with the Q-tip. Pugs can be touchy about your fussing with their nose wrinkles.

Clean the smaller wrinkles under your Pug's eyes in the same manner, and after you have dredged out his wrinkles, apply an astringent with a clean Q-tip to help keep them dry. If you notice bald spots or a rash in your Pug's wrinkles, take him to the veterinarian to determine whether he (your Pug) is growing a fungus.

Bathing Your Pug

Some people bathe their Pugs in the kitchen sink; others find it more comfortable to bathe their Pugs in the bathtub after they are fully grown. Whichever you prefer, a spray attachment is a necessity.

Before placing your Pug in the tub, gather up the supplies you will need for his bath.

Clean your Pug's ears if necessary before putting him into the tub, and put a small wad of cotton into each ear to prevent water from reaching the ear canal and possibly causing infection.

Protect your Pug's eyes against stray shampoo by putting a few drops of sterile eye ointment, available from any pharmacy, into each of them. If his face needs washing, attend to that, too, before you bathe him.

Put a rubber mat or a bath towel into the tub to provide secure footing for your Pug. Turn on the water and adjust the temperature,

clean your Pug's lower ear canal, buy a cleaning solution from your veterinarian and follow instructions faithfully.

If, when cleaning your Pug's ears, you discover a dark, granular, soil-like accumulation in his ear canal, he may have ear mites, the most common ear problem in dogs and cats. Generally, the more visible the dirt, the worse the infestation. Mites are contagious. They spread from one animal to another with whom it comes into close contact. If you suspect that your Pug has mites, schedule an appointment with your veterinarian.

Wrinkle-free Wrinkles

A Pug's facial wrinkles, because they are a dumping ground for excess food, tears, and eye gunk, can be a source of discomfort to

testing it with your wrist. If the water feels too warm to you, it probably will to your Pug. Adjust the temperature until the water is comfortably lukewarm. Make sure, too, that the house temperature is at least 72°F (22°C).

CHECKLIST

Bathing Supplies
✔ Brush(es)
✔ Shampoo
✔ Two or three bath towels
✔ Cotton balls
✔ Q-tips
✔ Mineral oil in a squeeze bottle
✔ Sterile eye ointment
✔ Hair dryer (optional)

Wet your Pug thoroughly after putting him into the tub, making sure the water penetrates to his skin, then apply the shampoo, lathering the coat generously. Do not lather past your Pug's neck. Allow the shampoo to remain in his coat for whatever length of time the manufacturer recommends before rinsing.

After your Pug has been lathered and rinsed—you are finished rinsing when the water coming off him is as clean as the water going onto him—remove him from the sink and wrap him in a towel. Use another towel to dry him more thoroughly.

Because baths are stimulating for Pugs, take your boy outside for a quick run after toweling him dry. Watching him race around in the low-rider crouch, which has to be seen to be appreciated, more than makes up for having to clean the mess in the bathroom and having to change your wet clothes.

FOOD FOR THOUGHT

You do not need to know the difference between a dispensable amino acid and an indispensable one in order to feed your Pug properly. All you need are some basic information and a few buying strategies.

Dog food is not hard to find. Supermarkets, convenience stores, pet shops, discount-buying clubs, websites, and veterinarians will gladly sell you all you need. The tricky part is sorting out dog-food manufacturers' claims about stronger bones, healthier teeth, and shinier coats.

Dry, Moist, or Semi-moist?

Dog food can be divided into three varieties according to its moisture content—dry, moist, and semi-moist. On average, dry foods contain 10 percent moisture; moist foods, also known as "canned" or "wet" foods, contain 75 percent; and semi-moist foods, 33 percent.

Dry foods—because of their lower cost, the convenience they provide, and the help they lend in controlling dental plaque—are most popular among dog owners. Canned foods are usually more appealing to dogs, in addition to being easier for them to eat because canned foods do not require as much chewing. Semi-moist foods, which rate high on the convenience and palatability scales, also rate high,

unfortunately, on the sugar, corn syrup, artificial colors, preservatives, and price scales.

Making Sense of Dog Food Labels

Reading a dog food label is like squinting at the last line on an eye-examination chart. You cannot be certain if you are seeing what you think you are seeing, and even when you are certain, you are reading letters, not words, letters such as *m-e-n-o-d-i-o-n-e s-o-d-i-u-m b-i-s-u-l-f-i-t-e*. Fortunately, the most significant part on a dog food label, the nutritional claim made by the manufacturer, is written in plain English.

Nutritional claims come in two varieties. In the first variety the manufacturer declares that "Bowser Bits" has been shown to provide complete and balanced nutrition in feeding trials conducted according to protocols established by the Association of American Feed Control Officials (AAFCO). In the second kind of nutritional claim the manufacturer attests that

"Bowser Bits" has been formulated to meet the various levels established in AAFCO's nutrient profiles.

In order to make the feeding-trials claim a manufacturer must compare data obtained from an experimental and a control group of dogs, each of which must contain at least eight members. The dogs in the experimental group are fed only "Bowser Bits" for a specified period of time, while the control group is fed a diet already known to be complete and balanced. At the end of the test period, if the dogs fed "Bowser Bits" do not differ significantly along certain variables from the control group, the manufacturer is entitled to claim that "Bowser Bits" provides complete and balanced nutrition according to AAFCO's feed-trial protocols. The variables on which the experimental and control groups are compared include weight, skin and coat condition, red blood-cell count, and other health measures.

In order to make the second kind of nutritional claim—that "Bowser Bits" was formulated to meet the levels established in AAFCO nutrient profiles—manufacturers must sign an affidavit stating that "Bowser Bits" was formulated from ingredients that will contain, after they have been processed, sufficient levels of all the nutrients AAFCO has determined a dog food should contain.

The difference between buying a dog food that has been tested in feed trials and one that has been formulated to meet AAFCO profiles is like the difference between buying a preferred stock and a futures option: the consumer can be more confident that the preferred stock—the feed-tested dog food—is going to perform the way it is supposed to perform because it has been fed to real dogs in real feeding trials.

The meets-the-nutrient-profiles statement, on the other hand, is misleading. It does not mean that AAFCO has analyzed the food in question and has certified that it meets organization standards. Nor does the statement necessarily mean that the manufacturer tested the food to determine whether it met AAFCO profiles. The meets-the-nutrient-profiles statement simply means the manufacturer formulated the food from ingredients that *should have* provided enough nutrients to meet the AAFCO profile. We say "should have" because cooking always destroys nutrients in dog food to some extent. Therefore, the nutrients that go into the kettle are always present in greater amounts than the nutrients that go into the food can.

All Stages

Thus far we have discussed only one part of the nutritional claim made on dog food labels, the part that tells you the basis on which manufacturers state their claims. There is, however, a second part to nutritional statements: the part that specifies the dogs for which the food is intended. Thus, a complete nutritional claim for a feed-tested food will say: "Animal feeding tests using AAFCO procedures substantiate that 'Bowser Bits' provides complete and balanced nutrition for all life stages of the dog." A complete nutritional claim for a meets-the-profile food will say: "'Bowser Bits' is formulated to meet the nutrient levels established by AAFCO nutrient profiles for all stages of a dog's life." Both these statements assure consumers that they can feed an all-life-stages food to their dogs from puppyhood through seniorhood, including motherhood, without worrying.

Adult Dogs Only and Other Stages

Instead of being formulated for all stages of a dog's life, some foods are intended for the maintenance of adult dogs only, and other foods are intended to support growth and reproduction. The latter, formulated to meet the increased nutritional needs of pregnant females and puppies, must contain more of certain nutrients—more protein, calcium, phosphorus, sodium, and chloride, for example—than maintenance foods do. Foods providing complete and balanced nutrition for all life stages of a dog also must meet growth and reproduction standards.

Seniors

In addition, many companies produce senior-citizen foods for older dogs. These foods, which must satisfy maintenance requirements in order to make the complete-and-balanced claim, are based on two principles: older dogs need less of certain nutrients—proteins, phosphorus, and salt, for example—than younger dogs require, and older dogs are less able to tolerate nutrient excess than younger dogs are.

Special Diets

Dogs are put on special diets for a number of reasons—illness, old age, or obesity among them. Dogs with hypertension, heart disease, or edema (swelling) should be on low-sodium diets. Dogs with kidney or liver conditions should be fed diets low in protein, phosphorus, and sodium. Dogs that are underweight or that suffer from pancreatic or liver disease should be fed highly digestible food. If your Pug is diagnosed with any of these or other conditions, your veterinarian may recommend a special diet. You should follow the veterinarian's instructions faithfully, and, of course, never feed a special diet to a Pug without first consulting a veterinarian.

Other special foods have been formulated to sculpt the overweight dog into a fit-and-trim specimen. Diet dog food, usually called "lite," allows you to feed the same amount of food while lowering a dog's caloric intake. Lite food contains 20 to 33 percent fewer calories than regular food does. Like other special diets, lite food should be fed only to those dogs for whom veterinarians recommend it.

Snacks and Treats

Roughly 20 cents of every dollar spent on dog food is spent on snacks or treats, but dog owners should remember that snacks and treats are not suitable for full-time use. If the

label on a package of snacks declares, "'Bowser Beef Wellington Bits' are intended for intermittent or supplemental use only," then use them intermittently. Do not allow snacks and treats to comprise more than 5 to 10 percent of your dog's diet. Your Pug is going to want snacks full-time if you offer them too frequently.

Chew Toys

Chew toys are based on the principle that a dog's teeth are certified erogenous zones. If you want to send a dog into terminal euphoria, bring home a sweaty, smoked-and-processed pig's ear, then set it on the floor. Within minutes your dog will have achieved a state of bliss known only to mystics and lottery winners.

Chewables, like any other source of pleasure, can also be a source of pain. Chicken bones should be avoided because they can splinter, get lodged in a dog's throat, or poke holes in his stomach or intestines. Harmful bacteria may

be lurking in knuckle or marrow bones; therefore, many dog owners recommend roasting them in a 175°F (79°C) oven for 20 minutes before serving.

Processed cowhide, generally known as rawhide, has been painted, processed, and pressed in "bones" for your dog's chewing enjoyment. In addition to being basted or broasted, some bones are infused with chicken, beef, hickory, cheese, peanut butter, or mint flavors, the latter for those Pugs who are expecting company. Because of its flexibility, rawhide also can be fashioned into surreal approximations of tacos, lollipops, cocktail franks, bagels, French fries, and giant pretzels to appeal to human tastes.

Be sure to monitor your Pug carefully the first few times you give him a rawhide chew toy. If he shows an inclination to chew off pieces of the toy, give him something more substantial to chew on instead, such as a bone made of hard nylon.

T I P

More Is Not Better

If a commercial dog food is labeled nutritionally complete and balanced, there is no reason to add vitamin or mineral supplements to it. Additional vitamins may upset the balance of vitamins already in the food and may cause vitamin toxicity. The only dogs needing vitamin or mineral supplements are those not eating properly because of illness or those losing increased amounts of body fluids because of diarrhea or increased urination. Dogs in either of those categories should be seen by a veterinarian, who may recommend a vitamin or mineral supplement.

All chewables should be served inside the house. A Pug gnawing happily on a chewy treat in the backyard will soon have his own posse of ants, flies, bees, if they are in season, and other uninvited vermin.

How Much and How Often to Feed

The amount of food a dog requires is determined by his age, condition, metabolism, environment, biological status, activity level, and ability to convert food into energy and heat. Variations in the effect of these factors among Pugs can make generalizations, not to mention feeding charts, something of a Pug in a poke.

Amounts

If there is one generalization to be made regarding dog food, it is this: the feeding

amounts recommended on dog food packages are too generous. Like the manufacturers of soap powder and shampoo, the makers of dog food usually overestimate the amount of their product a person needs to use in order to produce the desired results. This generosity on the part of dog food manufacturers is understandable: they would be embarrassed if dogs were to lose weight on the recommended amounts; therefore, they recommend high.

Pugs' food requirements diminish during their first year. From the age of three to six months, Pugs should eat three times a day. Each meal should consist, roughly, of 1/3 cup (79 ml) of dry puppy chow in a little warm tap water, and 1 or 2 tablespoons (15 ml) of canned all-life-stages or puppy food.

Pugs would happily observe this schedule the rest of their lives, but you should switch them to two meals a day when they are six months old. Each of those meals should comprise, roughly, 1/2 cup (118 ml) of dry puppy chow in a little warm tap water, and 1 or 2 tablespoons (15 ml) of canned all-life-stages food.

When your Pug celebrates his first birthday, switch to 1/2 cup (118 ml) of dry food (with water) designed for all life stages of a dog and 1 or 2 tablespoons (15 ml) of canned, all-life-stages food. As Pugs get older, they become more sedentary and they often gain weight. Older Pugs, those more than four years old, should get 1/3 cup (79 ml) of "lite" dry food, with warm tap water, and 1 or 2 tablespoons (15 ml) of canned food.

What Should a Pug Weigh?

According to the American Kennel Club breed standard, a Pug's "desirable" weight should fall between 14 and 18 pounds (6.3 to

8.2 kg), but this is not a reliable guide to any single Pug's ideal weight. Instead of looking at the scale to determine if your Pug exceeds or falls short of his desirable weight, look closely at him. If you can see his ribs, he's too skinny. If you run your hand gently down his back and you feel the spinous processes that stick out along his spine, or if you feel the transverse processes that protrude sideways from the spine, your Pug is too thin.

If your Pug has an hour-glass figure or if you cannot feel his ribs without a search warrant, he is too fat. Additional bouquets of fat are likely to blossom on the brisket (the area below the chest and between the forelegs), the neck, the abdomen, and the point at which the tail meets the body. If any of these spots seem too well padded, perhaps your Pug is too well fed.

TIP

Switching Diets

When you get your Pug, find out what kind of food he is used to eating. If that diet, whether commercial or homemade, is both sound for the puppy and convenient for you to feed, continue feeding it.

If you want to switch foods, which you probably will if you buy a puppy that has been raised on a homemade diet and you would prefer to leave the measuring and stirring to the pet food companies, add a suitable new food into the puppy's previous food in a one-part-new-to-three-parts-old ratio. Every three or four days increase the new food while decreasing the old until the changeover is complete.

If you cannot see your dog's ribs but you can feel them without having to squeeze his sides, he is probably neither too fat nor too thin.

Burdens of Excess Weight

There is a direct relationship between what you put into your Pug's bowl and the quantity of muscle and fat he develops. There also is a relationship between his weight and his state of health. Although excess weight often gets the blame for everything from heart problems to dislocated kneecaps, there is no denying that too much weight is often a contributing factor—and is almost always a complicating one—in many health-compromising conditions.

In addition to aggravating locomotor problems, excess weight will aggravate a collapsing trachea, an inherited condition common among toy breeds, in which the rings of cartilage in the windpipe collapse. Excess weight also makes it more difficult for Pugs to dissipate heat in warm weather, a problem already common to all members of the breed, fat or thin. Moreover, dogs, like people, are subject to an increasing litany of troubles as they grow older, and Pugs that are overweight when old age comes calling are saddled with an unfair handicap in fighting disease and infirmity.

It is difficult to specify the point at which a Pug's health could be compromised by surplus weight, but most females in excess of 19 pounds (8.6 kg) and most males in excess of 23 pounds (10.4 kg) are candidates for less food and more exercise.

THE HEALTHY PUG

Pugs tell us how they feel by the way they look and behave. When they are well, they display affection for their owners, a jolly approach to life, and a keen interest in mealtimes. When they are unwell, you and your veterinarian should conspire to make them well again.

Frequently, the first suggestion that a Pug is not feeling well is a lack of interest in food. If your Pug refuses a meal, or takes a few bites and stops eating, this might be cause for concern. If he skips two consecutive meals, call your veterinarian, who probably will want to know if your Pug's temperature is elevated or if he displays additional symptoms of illness such as vomiting or diarrhea.

Vaccinations

Until they are six to eight weeks old, puppies are protected from some diseases by the antibodies in their mothers' milk. Because this passive immunity interferes with puppies' ability to produce their own antibodies in response to vaccinations, they are not vaccinated for the first time until they are five or six weeks old.

The chart on the following page presents an overview of the vaccination process. Your veterinarian may adjust this schedule according to your puppy's needs and the disease threats present in your area.

The Importance of Booster Shots

A single vaccination does not make a puppy immune to diseases at once. Not for five to ten days, in fact, does a puppy's immune system begin to respond to the challenge posed by the antigens in a vaccine, and that response is low grade and not entirely effective. In addition we cannot be certain how long a puppy's passive immunity acquired from his mother will continue to compromise his ability to manufacture his own antibodies. That is why veterinarians revaccinate a puppy two, three, or four weeks after his initial vaccination; and many veterinarians re-revaccinate four weeks after the second vaccination, if not sooner.

Dogs should receive booster shots every year or every two to three years according to some veterinarians because antibodies decrease in number over time and the immune system

Puppy Vaccination Guidelines

Puppy's Age	Type of Vaccine Administered
5 weeks*	Parvovirus administered only if a puppy is at high risk for infection.
6 weeks*	Five-way combination vaccine that includes adenovirus cough, hepatitis, canine distemper, parainfluenza, and parvovirus vaccines. Some combination vaccines also may include leptospirosis and/or corona virus if those diseases are prevalent where the puppy lives.
9 weeks**	Same as six-week vaccine.
12 weeks	Same as six- and 12-week vaccine. Add Lyme vaccine if Lyme disease is a concern where the puppy lives or in an area to which he will be traveling.
12 to 16 weeks	Rabies vaccination as required by local ordinance.
15 weeks	A final dose of five- or seven-way vaccine.

*Should have been administered by a veterinarian at your puppy's breeder's request. Ask for vaccination certificate signed and dated by the administering veterinarian.
**If you purchased a puppy older than nine weeks of age, this vaccination should have been administered already. As before, ask for a signed and dated vaccination certificate.

⸺(HE(KLIST⸺

Potential Signs of Illness

Lack of interest in food is not the only, or always the first, sign of illness. You should call your veterinarian if your Pug exhibits any of the following symptoms:

- ✔ Difficult or labored breathing
- ✔ Temperature greater than 102.5°F (39.2°C) or less than 99°F (37.2°C)
- ✔ Persistent coughing, gagging, or sneezing
- ✔ Excessive drinking
- ✔ Repeated head shaking
- ✔ Runny, cloudy, or bloodshot eyes
- ✔ Runny nose
- ✔ Pale or inflamed gums
- ✔ Seriously foul breath
- ✔ Digging at or scratching his ears
- ✔ Bodily swelling or abscess
- ✔ Excessive scratching, licking, or chewing
- ✔ Noticeable flea dirt in his coat or bed
- ✔ Blood in his urine
- ✔ Blood or worms in his stool
- ✔ Limping or altered gait
- ✔ Dragging his hindquarters across the floor
- ✔ Appears lethargic for more than a day
- ✔ Recurring vomiting
- ✔ Diarrhea for more than one day
- ✔ Excessive drooling

needs to be stimulated to produce additional disease-fighting troops. Rabies boosters are given annually or every three years, depending on the type of vaccine administered.

External Parasites

The external parasites that can be found on a Pug include fleas, ticks, flies, mites, lice, and larvae. These hooligans not only damage skin tissue but also transmit harmful bacteria and/or viruses to your Pug. In sufficient quantities external parasites can sap a Pug's energy, weaken his resistance to infection, and saddle him with diseases and/or parasitic worms.

Signs that external parasites have been busy on your Pug include flea dirt, skin lesions, pustules, hair loss, dandruff, scaling, scabs, growths of thickened skin, and/or an unpleasant odor. If you notice any of these symptoms, or if your Pug begins to scratch or to bite at himself excessively, call your veterinarian. The earlier that external parasites are detected and confronted, the easier they are to control.

To check your Pug for fleas, turn him over and inspect the area near his hind legs, where his coat is thin. If you do not find any fleas but

Flea- and Tick-Fighting Products

Brand	Application	Targets	Effectiveness	Waterproof	Safety Range
Advantage®	Between shoulders	Fleas, flea larvae	1 month	Yes	8 weeks old and up
Frontline Plus®	Between shoulders	Fleas, flea larvae, ticks	1 month	Yes	8 weeks old and up
Frontline Top Spot®	Between shoulders	Fleas	1 month	Yes	8 weeks old and up
K9 Advantix®	Along the spine	Fleas, ticks, and mosquitoes	1 month	Yes	7 weeks old and up
Program®	Tablet taken orally with food	Prevents flea larvae and eggs from developing	1 month	N/A	6 weeks old and up
Revolution® available only by prescription from a veterinarian	Between shoulders	Fleas, ticks, heartworms, ear mites, sarcoptic mange	1 month	Yes	6 weeks old and up

you do find suspicious-looking specks of "dirt," put a small amount of that dirt on a paper towel and wet it. If the dirt turns red, it is flea dirt. You should run a flea comb through your Pug's coat to assess the situation.

Waging War on Fleas and Ticks

There are countless shampoos, sprays, powders, mousses, roll-ons, drop-ons, flea collars, wonder dips, and noise machines "guaranteed" to kill fleas and, in some cases, ticks. As of this writing (November 2009), researchers at Merck's laboratories had developed and tested a pill, derived from a substance found in a fun-

gus, that was effective in controlling fleas and ticks in dogs and cats for a full month without unfortunate side effects. According to one of the Merck researchers, this pill "has the potential to usher in a new era in the treatment of [ticks and fleas]." Meanwhile, the most current flea-and-tick fighters are listed in the table below. Before selecting any product, new or old, consult your veterinarian.

The Rest of the Story

Flea collars: Insecticidal flea collars do not win many flea-killing contests, and there is some concern that the pesticides in these collars can harm a dog. If you put a flea collar on your Pug, remove the collar from its package and snap the collar taut a few times to get rid of excess insecticide. Wash your hands immediately.

Let the collar air out away from pets and children for 24 to 36 hours before putting it on your dog. If he breaks out in sores or seems groggy or develops nasal irritation or inflamed eyes during the next few days, remove the collar and contact your veterinarian.

Flea collars that get wet must be removed and dried. Many collars are ineffective after they have been wet, and should be discarded.

The field: Among the more popular low-tech flea fighters is diatomaceous earth, which is sprinkled into rugs and upholstery on the theory that it causes fleas to dry up and die upon contact. Salt and 20 Mule Team Borax are also used for this purpose.

Brewer's yeast is added to a dog's food and dusted onto his coat and bedding because fleas so dislike its flavor they will seek other animals to bite after they have gotten a taste of it. Garlic, which is added to a dog's food, and vinegar, which is added to his drinking water, are reputed to have the same effect.

Chelated zinc, lecithin, cod liver oil, cold-pressed, unsaturated vegetable oil, kelp, and vitamin C also are touted as flea remedies. Scientists and most veterinarians, however, are skeptical about the value of many of these remedies.

Ticking Time Bombs

If you notice a bump on your Pug's skin that does not feel as though it ought to be there, part your dog's fur and have a look. If you discover a foul-looking, grayish lump, it is probably the body of a tick swollen with your dog's blood. Proceed to your dog-supplies drawer

and get the flea-removal tool you bought when you were shopping for puppy supplies.

Most flea-removal tools feature a hook that can be slid between the flea's face and your

TIP

Flea-fighting Strategies

If your Pug is overrun with fleas, bathe him with an anti-flea shampoo compatible with the anti-flea medication you have selected. Wash his bed and blankets, and vacuum the house thoroughly every other day until the fleas have been banished. Cut a flea collar into several pieces and put it in your vacuum-cleaner bag to challenge any fleas that wind up in there. Change the bag when it is half full in order to prevent a flea colony from sprouting in it.

Pug's skin without poking a hole in the latter. After the hook has been eased into place, give your wrist a turn upward and remove the tick.

What you do with the tick is your call. Fry it with a match, place it inside a folded paper towel and hammer it to death, whatever. Be creative and be quick, then get some alcohol and clean the spot where the flea had been attached to your Pug.

If you forgot to buy a flea-removal tool and you do not have a pair of Swiss Jeweler's Forceps #7 around the house, tweezers will do in a pinch; so will a hemostat. Be careful not to poke your Pug or to leave the tick's head attached after you have removed its swollen, disgusting body. A bodyless flea is still capable of causing infection.

Internal Parasites

Protozoa and worms are internal parasites often found in dogs. Protozoa are one-celled organisms that are free living and harmless for the most part. Some, however, can invade dogs and cats, causing a host of problems including severe diarrhea, which can lead to weight loss, debilitation, and sometimes death.

Giardiasis and Coccidiosis: The most common protozoan diseases found in dogs are giardiasis, caused by the *Giardia* species, and coccidiosis, most frequently caused by *Cystoisospora*. Their presence in a dog can be determined by a complete blood count, biochemical profile, and urinalysis. Other tests helpful in identifying the presence of protozoa include fecal evaluations and chest and abdominal X-rays. Depending on the protozoa involved, a veterinarian may prescribe antibiotics and specific deworming agents for an infected dog. In serious cases intensive support that includes fluids and blood transfusions may be necessary.

Worms: A Pug can play host to five kinds of worms: roundworms, hookworms, whipworms, tapeworms, and heartworms. The presence of

Take It to Heart

The mosquitoes that transmit heartworms require sufficiently warm temperatures over a sufficient period of time to work their magic. There is a formula for determining when that tipping point has been reached, but it involves, among other calculations, keeping track of the number of days in a 30-day period on which the temperature has risen above 57°F (13.9°C). Not surprisingly, most dog owners, particularly those living in temperate climates, prefer to use a heartworm preventive all year regardless of temperature.

roundworms, hookworms, and whipworms can be detected through stool-sample analysis. Tapeworms can best be identified by lifting your dog's tail and peering studiously at his butt in search of small, white tapeworm segments that look like rice. These segments also can be seen on fresh stools. The presence of heartworms can be detected by blood-sample analysis.

Heartworms: Heartworms, one of the most prevalent and dangerous diseases in dogs, are spread by mosquitoes. Fortunately, heartworm-preventive medications are available that kill larval heartworms in dogs. If your Pug is negative for heartworms, your veterinarian has several options for keeping him that way: pills or topical applications administered once a month or an injectable product administered every six months. If your Pug tests positive for heart-

worms, he will require treatment that may include hospitalization and/or surgery.

Most worms are not difficult to control. When you acquire a Pug, ask the person from whom you get him when he (the Pug) was last dewormed and what deworming agent he was given. To be safe, take a stool sample and your new Pug's deworming history to your veterinarian, who will recommend a safe, effective deworming agent and will set up a deworming schedule.

Keeping the Pearly Gates Pearly

Clean teeth may help to prevent certain diseases of the heart, liver, and kidneys that are thought to be caused by the spread of bacteria from a dog's mouth. Diligent Pug owners, therefore, do not allow poor dental hygiene to put the bite on their dogs' health.

Dry dog foods, which ought to make up the bulk of a Pug's diet (see *Food for Thought*, page 39), help to some extent to reduce plaque (the sticky combination of bacteria, food particles, and saliva that is constantly forming and hardening on teeth). Unfortunately, the carbohydrates in dry foods stick to the teeth and act as compost for the bacteria that is plaque's main ingredient. Canned dog foods, for their part, do nothing to remove plaque, and the sugar they contain adds to its buildup.

If plaque is not removed regularly from your Pug's teeth, it hardens into tartar and intrudes itself between teeth and gums, creating a tiny sinkhole in which bacteria multiply. These bacteria invade the gingiva (gum), causing it to become inflamed, to swell, and to bleed when probed. This condition, known as **gingivitis**, is

reversible if treated early. If not, it escalates into **periodontitis**—ulceration of the gums and erosion of the alveolar bone, which holds the teeth in place. Periodontitis is not reversible, and if it is not controlled, the gums and alveolar bone eventually become so eroded that the teeth fall out.

To check for signs of gingivitis, hold your Pug's head with one hand and lift his upper lip along one side of his mouth with the other hand. Look closely at his teeth and gums. Repeat this procedure on the opposite side and in the front of his mouth; then inspect his bottom teeth. If there is a red line anywhere along his gums, make an appointment to have your veterinarian check your Pug's teeth.

Signs of Oral Disease

Other signs of oral disease include perpetual morning breath, avoidance of dry food, resistance to being stroked on the muzzle, brown or yellow crust on tooth surfaces, loss of appetite, and drooling. If your dog exhibits any of these symptoms, schedule an appointment with your veterinarian.

Chewing

Pugs are happy to assist in their own dental care by chewing on rawhide bones, knuckle bones, marrow bones, or bones made of hard nylon. Encourage this participation by giving your Pug some kind of bone to floss with on a regular basis.

Brushing

You can assist your Pug in keeping his teeth clean by brushing them once or twice a week. Introduce this idea gradually. Begin by looking at your Pug's teeth as you did during the gingivitis inspection, but instead of just looking, rub a finger along his teeth, first in front of them and then behind them.

When your Pug is used to this routine, substitute a soft-bristle, child's toothbrush or a finger brush made especially for dogs in place of your finger. You will want to add canine toothpaste to whatever brush you choose. Your veterinarian will be able to recommend a suitable one.

Medicating and Feeding a Sick Pug

Ignorance is bliss when medicating a Pug. As long as he remains ignorant of the pill or powder hidden in the food you offer him, he will swallow it blissfully. If your Pug is too sick to eat, pills may have to be administered manually or with a pill gun. The latter is available in a pet shop, a pet supply catalog, or an Internet site (see Information, page 92). In any event, the technique is the same: place the pill as far back on your Pug's tongue as possible, hold his mouth shut, and stroke his throat until he swallows. Praise him when he does.

Fluids: Pugs convalescing from an illness or injury must consume enough fluid to replace what they lose through elimination and panting. If your Pug is unwilling to drink, you will have to get nourishing liquids—water or broths—down his throat one way or another.

Spooning fluid into a Pug's mouth can be messy. A syringe or a spray bottle is a bet-

CAUTION

The Wrong Stuff

Never use human toothpaste on your dog's teeth. The foaming agent it contains can set off gastric problems in dogs. Also avoid using baking soda or salt to clean your dog's teeth. These substances do not remove plaque effectively, and they contain sodium, which can be harmful to older dogs with heart disease.

ter choice. Your veterinarian can tell you how much fluid your Pug should receive daily.

Food: If your Pug is off his feed, switch to an all-canned-food diet and warm his food slightly in the microwave to release its aromas before giving it to him. Stir the warmed food, and test it with a finger for pockets of heat before offering it to your Pug.

When a Pug is not eating, virtually any food is nutritious food for the time being. Baby food, turkey or chicken from the deli, canned dog food marinated in beef or chicken broth, hamburger seasoned with garlic, broth straight up, anything that will revive your Pug's interest in eating. In serious cases you may have to feed your Pug a pureed diet with a large syringe.

Exercise

Although Pugs do not require much exercise, they should be provided with a securely fenced yard in which they can race about when the spirit moves them. They need not spend long amounts of time in the yard. An hour or so in the morning and again in the afternoon, weather permitting, are sufficient—with access to fresh water, of course.

Pugs without access to a yard should be walked 15 or 20 minutes at least once a day, in addition to their constitutional walks. If possible, take your Pug to an area where he can enjoy a good run under your supervision two or three times a week.

Inherited Problems in Pugs

Like all pedigreed dogs, Pugs are subject to a number of inherited disease conditions. The following are the ones most frequently encountered:

Legg-Perthes is a degeneration of the head of the femur bone, the long upper bone of the hind leg. Legg-Perthes can be corrected by surgery.

Luxating patella is a dislocation of the patella, the small, flat, moveable bone at the front of the knee. A Pug with luxating patella favors his affected leg when he walks, and when he runs, he lifts it, setting it down only every few steps. The tendency to luxating patella is inherited, but excess weight can aggravate that tendency. Luxating patella can be corrected by surgery.

Pug dog encephalitis is an inflammation of the brain that is unique to Pugs. Seizure is the primary symptom of Pug dog encephalitis, which tends to affect young to middle-aged Pugs. Seizures are preceded sometimes by periods of lethargy and loss of muscle coordination. Other signs include agitation, aggression, pacing in circles, and pressing the head against objects.

Pugs with the slow, progressive form of encephalitis will return to normal between seizures, which reoccur in a few days or a few weeks. Pugs with the acute, rapidly progressing form of the disease walk abnormally and appear depressed and bewildered between seizures.

Phenobarbital helps to control seizures; corticosteroids help to reduce the inflammation of the brain; antibiotics can provide some relief if there is a bacterial component to the disease, but there is no cure for Pug dog encephalitis.

Progressive retinal atrophy (PRA) is the wasting away of the vessels in the retina, the innermost coat of the posterior part of the eyeball. PRA is manifest initially as night blindness in young dogs. As the disease progresses, its victims become blind.

Entropion is an inversion of the eyelid that usually affects the lower lid. Entropion, which can be corrected by surgery, causes persistent irritation of the cornea.

Pigmentary keratitis is the deposition of pigment or melanin on the surface of the eye

by the cornea in response to unrelieved irritation and/or inflammation. The Pug's shallow eye sockets can cause the eyes to protrude, and if they protrude too much, the eyelids cannot fully cover and protect the cornea, nor can they distribute a tear film effectively over the entire surface of the eye. This condition is known as lagophthalmos, and it is one of the causes of prolapsed eyes and of dry eye or keratoconjunctivitis (KCS). Other irritating factors include ingrown eyelashes (trichiasis), aberrant eyelid hairs (distichiasis), and trauma to the eye.

Pigmentary keratitis can be permanent if the cause of the irritation or inflammation is not removed—by surgery if necessary—be it excessive nasal fold tissue, ingrown hairs, or KCS. After the cause of the problem has been eliminated, superficial deposits of pigment can be treated with topical eye medications. Pigment deep within the cornea may not be so easily treated, and if it impairs a Pug's vision, it should be removed surgically.

Elongated soft palate, which occurs in short-faced breeds, often results in some degree of obstruction of the dog's airway. This obstruction leads to snorting, snoring, and breathing through the mouth. If your Pug begins to honk like a goose, put his head back, and gasp for air, consult your veterinarian to see if he or she considers your Pug a candidate for corrective surgery.

Stenotic nares, a birth defect found in short-nosed breeds, is caused by nasal cartilage that is too soft. Stenotic nares, literally "narrow nostrils," collapse when a dog inhales. This prevents him from drawing in air. Dogs with this condition produce a foamy-looking nasal discharge, and they breathe through their mouths when excited. Stenotic nares can be corrected surgically.

In case of an emergency, you may need more in your first-aid kit than a towel and your veterinarian's phone number. The following is a checklist of first-aid items you should keep on hand.

First-Aid Kit
✔ Blanket
✔ Gauze sponges
✔ Roll of narrow gauze
✔ Roll of bandages, such as a gauze wrap that stretches and clings
✔ Adhesive tape, hypo-allergenic
✔ Nonadherent sterile pads
✔ Pediatric rectal thermom-eter
✔ Three percent hydrogen peroxide
✔ Topical antibiotic oint-ment
✔ Baby-dose syringe or eye dropper (unbreakable)
✔ Sterile saline eyewash
✔ Children's aspirin (81 mg tablet); use for fever or pain as directed by your veterinarian
✔ Petroleum jelly
✔ National Animal Poison Control Center telephone number (1-888-426-4435)
✔ Activated charcoal for use in case of poisoning
✔ Cotton balls
✔ Rubber gloves

✔ Syringes in 3-, 6-, and 12-cm sizes for feeding and medicating
✔ Artificial tears
✔ Small scissors
✔ Water-based sterile lubri-cant
✔ Rubbing alcohol
✔ Epsom salts
✔ Sterile eye lubricant
✔ Styptic powder or pencil to stop bleeding from minor cuts
✔ Hydrocortisone ointment
✔ Veterinary first-aid manual
✔ Your veterinarian's and the local emergency animal hos-pital's phone numbers

Practicing for Emergencies
In some emergencies you may need to take your Pug's temperature and/or pulse. You will be better prepared—and less anxious—if you have done so before in a nonemergency situation.

Inserting a rectal ther-mometer is a straightforward proposition; taking your dog's pulse, not so much. You may be able to feel his pulse, which occurs with every heartbeat, by placing your hand low on his chest, near the elbow joint. You can feel his pulse also through the femoral artery, high on the inside of his thigh. Place two

fingers on the middle of the thigh close to the place where his leg joins his body.

After you have located a pulse, count the number of beats you feel in 15 seconds, then multiply by four to determine your dog's pulse rate. The normal pulse rate for a dog ranges from 70 to 180 beats per minute. Generally, the larger the dog, the slower the pulse.

Fashioning an Emergency Muzzle
Should misfortune befall your Pug, do not contribute to it by dancing around hys-terically and/or screeching in a high-pitched voice. Keep yourself and your dog calm, call the veterinarian, and fol-low instructions carefully. If you are afraid your Pug may bite, fashion a muzzle from a strip of gauze. Tie a loose single knot in the center of the gauze and slide the loop over your Pug's muzzle so that the knot is under his chin. Pull the loop until it fits snugly over the muzzle, then draw the ends of the gauze behind your Pug's ears and secure the makeshift muzzle with another single knot.

EMERGENCY

Heatstroke

A Pug's temperature, taken rectally, ranges between 100 and 102.5°F (37.8 and 39.2°C). Moderate heatstroke occurs when his temperature registers between 104 and 106°F (40 to 40.1°C). A Pug can recover from moderate heatstroke within an hour if he receives prompt first aid. If his temperature exceeds 106°F (40.1°C), the consequences can be deadly and immediate veterinary assistance is critical.

Heatstroke destroys cell membranes and leads to organ failures. The dehydration that accompanies heatstrokes thickens the blood, thereby depriving tissues of necessary oxygen. The muscles, kidneys, liver, and gastrointestinal tract also may be affected. Moreover, heatstroke can cause swelling and subsequent damage to the brain, blindness, hemorrhages, convulsions, and fatal seizures.

If your Pug becomes overheated and pants excessively after being outdoors—behaviors that may be accompanied by vomiting, diarrhea, collapse, hot and dry skin, and/or pale lips—take his temperature at once. If his temperature is elevated, between 104 and 106°F (40 to 40.1°C), and if he is able to drink, give him small amounts of cold water. Next try to reduce his temperature slowly with a cold, but not ice cold, water bath. Move his legs gently to increase circulation. Take his temperature every 15 minutes until it drops below 103°F (39.4°C) and remains there.

Poisoning

Curiosity can be fatal not only to cats but also to your Pug. The chances of your Pug getting into some kind of poison-related mischief, in such places as the cabinet under the kitchen sink, will be greatly reduced if you are diligent

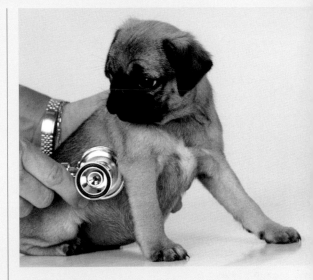

in Pug-proofing your house (see page 24). If you suspect that your Pug has been poisoned despite your best precautionary efforts—if, for example, he is drooling, vomiting, breathing slowly, or is suffering from abdominal pain or diarrhea—call your veterinarian to let him or her know you are on your way.

If you know what your Pug was eating before he went all wobbly, take a sample of it to the veterinarian's with you. If you do not know what your Pug ate but he has vomited, take a sample of that instead.

If, and only if, you know that your dog has eaten a specific plant or food—or he has licked anti-freeze off the garage floor— just immediately before getting sick, give him one to two teaspoons of hydrogen peroxide every five minutes until he vomits. If he does not vomit within 15 minutes, call your veterinarian. Do not induce vomiting if you do not know what your Pug ate. The ingredients in many household cleaners cause additional harm when vomited.

UNDERSTANDING YOUR PUG

There is no better company on two legs or four than a Pug dog. No friend is more loyal, no comrade more jolly, no confidant more trustworthy.

Pugs are excellent at keeping secrets, keeping us amused, and keeping loneliness at bay. Your Pug will always be ready to lick your face when the muddy footprints of a frustrating day are stamped across your brow. When you are ticked off because of something the boss, the clerk at the convenience store, the person in the next cubicle at work, the president, some editorial writer, a loved one, the neighbor's kid, or some fool on the Internet said or did recently, your Pug will be happy to sit and listen to you complain about the unfairness of it all. If you are a good Pug owner, you will be ready to return the favor. We should comfort Pugs for being dogs as much as they comfort us for being human.

A Pug's View of the World

Although Pugs are often referred to as "little people in fur," they are wired up differently than we are. By the time they are four weeks old, their senses and their ability to communicate are functioning at near-adult capacity, and they are capable of interacting socially with other dogs and with humans. When your Pug puppy arrives at your house at 10 to 12 weeks of age, he is not really a puppy but a dog in disguise.

Smell

Unlike the human brain, which is dominated by the visual cortex, the Pug's brain is dominated by the olfactory cortex, which is roughly 40 times larger in Pugs than it is in humans. In addition, the surface area of a Pug's nasal membranes is the size of a handkerchief while a human's is no bigger than a postage stamp. Not surprisingly the five million primary receptor cells in the human nose are mocked by the 125 to 300 million primary receptor cells in a dog's nose, depending on his breed. That is

why dogs can sense odors at concentrations nearly 100 million times lower than humans can—a drop of perfume in five quarts of water, for example. Because breeds with longer noses have the best sense of smell, Pugs and other brachycephalic (short-face) breeds are closer to the 125-million-primary-receptor-cell floor than they are to the 300-million-cell ceiling. Nevertheless, their sense of smell is way superior to ours.

Taste

A Pug will eat almost anything because of his relative lack of taste buds, not his lack of taste. Dogs have fewer taste buds, approximately 1,700, than we humans have, approximately 9,000. Moreover, a dog's taste buds are clustered near the tip of his tongue, the area on which food spends the least amount of time.

Because a Pug is guided more by his sense of smell than his sense of taste, he will eat, even if he is not feeling well, as long as he can smell his food. This is why we feed sick Pugs with strong-smelling or strongly seasoned foods or with food that has been warmed slightly in the microwave to kick-start its flavor.

— FUN FACT —

Scents Alive

When a dog breathes normally, air does not pass directly over his scent receptors, which are located near the back of his nose; but if he takes a deep whiff, the air drawn into his nose triggers those receptors.

─── fUN fACT ───

Ears Looking at You

Dogs possess 18 or so muscles that enable them to swivel, tilt, raise, ratchet, or lower their ears in order to locate and to capture sound more efficiently, and in a pinch they can also do that head-tilt thing. We are stuck with cupping an ear and asking "say again?" A Pug's conformation puts him up against it in hearing contests with other dogs, however, because breeds with erect ears hear better than those with floppy ones.

Hearing

Just about anything you can hear, your Pug can hear better. In addition, he can detect fainter sounds from greater distances, up to four times as great, than you can, and at much higher frequencies.

A dog's frequency range is approximately 40 Hz to 60,000 Hz. A Hz (hertz) is one cycle (sound vibration) per second. The human frequency range is 20 Hz to 20,000 Hz. We may outperform dogs in detecting low, rumbling bass notes oozing from a car stereo two traffic lights behind us, but dogs box our ears at the other end of the audio spectrum. (A dog's hearing is keen enough to detect a mouse singing falsetto half a mile away.) Furthermore, dogs are able to determine the direction a sound is coming from much more accurately than we can, and they can differentiate between similar sounds better than we can, too.

Touch

Touch is the first sense that a dog develops. Mothers begin touching their puppies almost immediately after they are born, and puppies, for their part, thrive on their mothers' licking and nuzzling. The comfort that Pugs derive from contact during infancy leads them to seek contact with other dogs and with humans throughout life. In fact, touch can have a calming effect on a dog's heart rate, as it can on ours.

Although body sensitivity varies among dogs, most enjoy being petted around the head, chest, back, and, if they roll over onto their backs as you are petting them, on their bellies as well. The most sensitive nerve endings are found along the spine and toward the tail.

Sight

The retina—in humans and in canines—is lined with two kinds of photoreceptors: rods and cones. Rods are far more numerous than cones in both species, but even more so in dogs than in humans. Rods work best in low light and in the detection of motion. That is why dogs see better at night than we do. Rods, however, are not sensitive to color.

Dogs are color-blind to an extent. A dog's visual world consists of yellows, blues, and grays. What we perceive as red appears as yellow to a dog, while anything that is green to us is white, a shade of gray, to him. Therefore, the grass is not always greener on the other side to a Pug; it is, rather, a whiter shade of pale.

Dogs are not at a disadvantage for not being able to see all the colors of the spectrum. During the course of evolution dogs and humans each developed the visual system that worked best for them. Dogs were not diurnal (of or

Seeing the Small Picture

A dog's visual acuity—his ability to see details—is roughly six times poorer than the average human's. Visual acuity, measured in cycles per degree, is an assessment of the number of lines that can be seen as distinct entities in the visual field. Humans can see approximately 30 cycles per degree while dogs can see roughly 12.

belonging to the daytime) until we domesticated them. The ability to see at night, therefore, was far more important to the dog than the ability to detect color. Their prey is often

camouflaged by its surroundings, so dogs are unable to rely on color vision cues as heavily as humans do to find their food, which is usually hidden in plain view on brightly lit supermarket shelves.

Another reason that dogs see much better at night than humans do is the mirrorlike tissue in canine eyes. This tissue enhances night vision by reflecting incoming light back through the retina, re-stimulating the eyes' light-sensing cells and boosting their signal to the brain. You can demonstrate the effect of this mirrolike tissue by shining a flashlight in your Pug's eyes at night. The reflected light gleaming back at you is known as "eyeshine."

Dogs have a wider field of vision than humans do and a better ability to detect motion at the horizon. A dog can recognize moving objects nearly half a mile (0.8 km) away, while humans often fail to see that the car in front of them has stopped to make a left-hand turn.

How Pugs Perceive Humans

Pugs know more about us than they let on. They may not write people-care manuals, but they read us like books nonetheless. Here are the fruits of their observations.

The Indulgent Owner

Allows his or her Pug to do whatever he wants for fear that asking him never mind telling him to behave will break his spirit or cause him not to love his owner. Winds up with a hyperactive, out-of-control dog who does not love his owner anyway because who loves a doormat?

The Unpredictable Owner

Never reacts the same way twice from one day to the next. It's okay to jump into the owner's lap today because the owner is wearing jeans, but it will not be okay tomorrow when the owner gets home from work in a power suit. The owner cannot decide whether to allow the Pug to sleep on the sofa or not, then finally decides he is allowed to sleep on the sofa if his feet are clean. What do Pugs know from clean feet?

The Absentee Owner

Is seldom home except when she is sleeping. If the owner had a clue, she would find the Pug a better home and get herself a Chia pet.

The Contrite Owner

Yesterday this owner had only an hour to spend with the Pug, so today she follows him around constantly, even cooks him something fabulous to eat. Tomorrow it is dry kibble again, and maybe an upset stomach from yesterday's foie gras.

Communicating with Your Pug

There might be a language barrier between us and our dogs, but that does not mean there has to be a communication barrier. Pugs are able to let us know what they want. With a little practice and equal persistence, we can make that a two-way conversation.

Voice

Pugs can accumulate a significant working vocabulary, but we communicate with them more through vocal tone and volume than we do through definitions.

If, for example, you say "Etslay ogay, oybay" in a bright, cheery tone when you get your Pug's leash, he is going to react with the same enthusiasm as if you had said, "*Let's go, boy*"; but if you say "*Let's go, boy*" in the stern, disapproving tone you use to say "*Stop*" when you find him devouring something he shouldn't, he is apt to cringe instead.

All dogs are Pavlov's dog when it comes to learning vocabulary. If you want to teach your Pug the meaning of a word or phrase, link it to an action. If you say, "*Let's go out, dude*" before getting your Pug's leash, in relatively short order all you have to do is say, "*Let's go*

out" and he is off the couch and heading for the door.

Hands

Most if not all Pug puppies see hands as something on which to chew, but eventually they associate hands with other functions: petting, food delivery, grooming, and taking stuff out of their mouths. They are, accordingly, disposed to viewing human hands as their ten-fingered friends, who for some reason do not want them chewing on shoes.

We let our fingers do the talking whenever we touch our Pugs. That talking should be done in a gentle tone of voice, one that communicates loving kindness. If we use our hands to communicate displeasure, either implied or inflicted, our dogs are likely to become hand shy, i.e., to crouch warily if someone tries to pet them. How embarrassing is *that* down at the dog park?

Dog-behavior experts are of two minds on the subject of hand corrections. Some rank hand corrections right up there with child abuse, maybe higher, but others say it is not the use of hands but the way in which we use them that does harm. These experts teach restraint in the use of hands—a quick, light "pop" under the chin or a soft but notice-able jab in the shoulder with the fingers of one hand held straight and pointing in the shoulder's direction. These experts also cau-tion against ever striking a dog from above or behind. If you follow their guidelines, you can use hand corrections on your dog when he is being truly obnoxious.

Facial Expressions

According to a study reported in the October 2008 edition of *New Scientist*, dogs do not read our emotions so much as they read our faces. The study, led by Dr. Kin Guo of the University of Lincoln in the U.K., was based on a phenomenon called "left gaze bias."

Prior to this study, research had demon-strated that human faces are lopsided when displaying emotion. The right side of the face, which is controlled by the left side of the brain, more clearly expresses emotion because emotion is the province of the brain's left side. Meanwhile, the left side of the human face, controlled by the buttoned-down right side of the brain, is more devoid of emotion. Therefore, when we meet someone, we tend to direct our attention to the left (the other person's right side) because that is where the clues to that person's emotional state are displayed. The Lincoln University researchers

found that dogs do the same thing when look-ing at people.

The 17 dogs that participated in the study were shown images of human faces, dog faces, monkey faces, and inanimate objects. Each dog's eye and head movements were videotaped as he looked at the images. These movements suggested that dogs recognized the human faces and that their eyes drifted left when looking at people just as our eyes do when we meet someone. Interestingly, the dogs in the study did not look left when they were shown images of animals or inanimate objects. No other animal has been found to display this behavior before.

Dr. Guo theorized that over thousands of generations of association with humans, dogs may have evolved left gaze bias as a way to gauge our emotions.

Body Language

Although scientists are still struggling to figure out why dogs have the ability to read human body language, Pug owners have known this for a long time. Our movements and gestures, no matter how subtle, reveal much about what we are going to do next; and if that involves our dogs, they are on the case. That is why if we are sitting in the kitchen and look toward the hook where the dog's leash is hanging, he is at the door.

Pugs also are able to read displeasure in our body movements. If your Pug begins jump-ing up and putting his paws on you when you return home, simply turn and walk away with-out acknowledging him. Eventually, when you return home, he will manage his enthusiasm better.

OBEDIENCE TRAINING

Every pack must have a leader. If you do not want the job, your Pug will take it. When you allow this to happen, you are not the alpha dog, and, as the joke about sled dogs goes, the scenery never changes for followers.

Dogs always have depended on the ability to function within a social hierarchy in order to survive. In the wild—a concept difficult to entertain regarding Pugs—dogs and their wolfish ancestors live in packs dominated by the alpha member, or leader, of the pack. The alpha dog, generally a female, is judge, jury, sheriff, exalted ruler, and high priestess of the pack. When the alpha dog wants to rest, the other members of the pack lie down. When the alpha dog wants to move on, the pack follows. When the alpha dog wants to hunt, the pack members sharpen their fangs.

Your Pug's ability to thrive in a follow-the-leader arrangement makes him inclined to seek your approval, and makes it possible for you to assume the role of the alpha dog in his life. This principle also makes it possible for 18-pound (8.2-kg) dogs to dominate people who are much larger—and often more intelligent—than they are. Just as nature abhors a vacuum, pack animals abhor a democracy.

Teaching Your Pug His Name

If your Pug has a name when you acquire him, and if he responds to that name, let him keep it. You may shorten it if you want, but your Pug will have enough to do adjusting to a new home without having to adjust to a new identity as well.

If your Pug does not have a name, you can teach him to respond to whatever name you choose by praising him every time he does. Suppose, for example, you have decided to name your Pug "Buster." While you are playing with him, or just sitting quietly with him, say his name enthusiastically. If he looks in any direction but yours, do nothing. Wait a bit, then say his name again. Buster will look toward you eventually. When he does, say "*Good*" and praise him.

Now you have Buster's attention, which is all you want at this point. He does not have

Training Tips

1. Keep training sessions brief at first: two five-minute sessions a day, with several hours' break in between, are better than one ten-minute session.

2. Do not scold your Pug, by name or otherwise, if he makes a mistake. Show him by voice and example what you want him to do.

3. Limit your Pug to one teacher.

4. If your Pug attempts to bolt during a training session, say nothing. Bring him back quietly and try again. A training session is not finished until you say it is.

5. Let other members of the household know that you do not wish to be disturbed during a training session.

6. If your Pug is not catching on to a lesson as quickly as you would like, what are you doing wrong? Are you going too quickly? Are you handling him too abruptly? Are you speaking to him harshly? Are you rewarding him as soon as he does the right thing? Maybe it is time to take a step back and go over a routine he already knows for a day or two in order to build up his confidence before coming back to the lesson that is giving him trouble.

to stop what he is doing and come to you when he hears his name, but he should look in your direction as if to say, "OK, I'm listening. What's up?"

Wait a minute or two and say Buster's name again. You may have to say it two or even three times more, but if you put enough enthusiasm into your tone, Buster *will* look at you. When he does, make a fuss over him again. After he has responded to his name three or four times in one session, you have accomplished your mission. If you repeat that mission two or three times a day for a week or so, you will have Buster's ear anytime you call his name, and he will come to realize that the sound of those two syllables has a special meaning all its own.

Come

The first command you should teach your Pug is to come when he is called. Once he has learned to respond to this command virtually without fail, you will have established a significant measure of control over him, a control that could serve him well in times of trouble. What is more, the confidence you will have acquired in teaching your Pug to come when you call will give you more confidence in teaching him additional commands.

After Buster has learned to respond to his name, pick a room in your house, put a leash on Buster, and let him wander around investigating. In a minute or two say *"Buster, come"* in a happy, excited tone. You may reinforce

this command at first by patting your leg and/ or stepping backward.

If Buster hustles over to see what you want, praise him, give him a treat, and let him go back to what he was doing. If he ignores you, tug lightly on the leash to encourage him. If he still ignores you, pick him up, carry him to the spot from which you called him, and praise him, but do not give him a treat. Try again in a few minutes.

Within days Buster should come reliably when he is called. Then try calling him when you are in the same room but he is not wear- ing a leash. The house rules still apply: if Buster

TIP

Keep Smiling

Although Pugs can be single minded, they are eager to please and able to learn. You should bring the same attitude to each training session. Do not begin training if you are out of sorts. Chop wood, go jogging, work out for half an hour, or put on the headphones. Leave the training for another day.

comes when he is called, he gets a treat; if he ignores you, pick him up, carry him to the spot from which you called him, and toss him a few *attaboys*, but withhold the treat.

After Buster is coming to you consistently when you call, increase the distance between you and him by gradual increments: first, to 4 or 5 feet (1.22–1.5 m) for several days and then to 6 or 7 feet (1.5–2.1 m) for several days. Keep increasing the distance between you and him until he responds to your command from across the room.

When Buster comes when he is called off leash indoors, practice this command outside. If Buster decides coming when he is called is an indoor activity, you will need a long, retractable leash as a training aid.

From your Pug's point of view, there are only two reasons for coming when he is called: praise and food. Consequently you never should call him when you want to scold him, give him medication that is not hidden in food, or do anything else that might cause him discomfort. If he associates a summons with an unpleasant consequence, he will begin ignoring all summonses.

After Buster has learned to come faithfully when you call, you can reduce the lavish praise to a simple *"Good boy"* or a pat on the head by way of intermittent reinforcement. Do not eliminate the reinforcement altogether or you risk eliminating his willing response.

Sit

Stand facing Buster and hold a treat in your right hand at the level of his nose. As soon as he shows any interest in the treat, move your treat hand in an arc past his eyes

TIP

Intermittent Reinforcement

After your Pug has begun to respond to a command, do not give him a food reward every time he does. If he knows he can get a treat every time, he may decide on occasion that it is more rewarding to continue what he was doing, even if he was doing nothing, than to get that old, predictable treat; but if he does not get a treat every time, he will not be certain that treats are always in store. Therefore, he will be more likely to answer every time because he always will be hoping a treat is forthcoming.

Psychologists call this maybe-yes, maybe-no technique *intermittent reinforcement.* They caution, however, that the schedule of intermittent reinforcement must not be predictable. If you withhold the treat every third time you summon Buster, he will soon begin timing his refusals to coincide with the empty hand. To be effective, intermittent reinforcement must be random. If your training sessions consist of four or five practices of the *come* command during two or three sessions a day, withhold the treat the second time you call Buster during the first session, the fourth time during the second session, and so on.

Do not be intermittent with your praise, however. You do not want Buster thinking that you love him less for some performances than for others. Every time he comes when you call, say *"Good boy,"* even if you do not give him a treat.

toward the top of his head. As your hand moves, Buster more than likely will raise his head to follow the progress of the treat; and, in a perfect world, he will sit down naturally as a result of raising his head. Right before his butt touches the ground, say *"Sit"* once and reward him with the treat after he touches down.

If Buster backs away from you in order to get a better look at the treat, take a step or two away from him, show him the treat, and repeat the exercise. Be careful not to say *"Sit"* again until right before he has done so.

If Buster still does not sit, show him what you want him to do. Take his collar in one hand and, as you are pulling up on the collar, say *"Sit"* and push down on his rump with your other hand until he assumes the sitting position. Give him the treat, and after he has been sitting pretty for a few seconds, say *"OK"* to let him know that it is all right for him to stand up.

Stay

To teach the *stay* command, put your Pug in a sitting position on your left. With the leash in your left hand, lean down and place your right hand—palm toward your dog—about 6 inches (15 cm) in front of his face. Say *"Stay"* and, after you do, move slowly until you are facing your dog from a distance of 2 or 3 feet (.61–.91 cm). The leash still will be in your left hand at this point, so if Buster begins to move toward you, repeat the *stay* command and pull the leash straight up gently.

Clicker Training

Clicker training is based on pairing the sound of a clicker—available for $2 to $4 at a pet store—with the arrival of a treat. You can accomplish this by clicking your clicker one time, then tossing your Pug a treat immediately. After several trials repeated across several days, he will begin to expect a treat whenever he hears the clicker.

Because his little Pug brain also will associate whatever he was doing before he heard the click with the reward that followed it, do not click when he is doing something mischievous. Click only when he is doing something neutral such as sitting quietly in a room with you.

After your Pug has connected the sound of the clicker with the arrival of a treat, use the clicker to reinforce desired behavior as soon as it happens during training. In teaching your Pug to sit, for example, use the clicker instead of your voice to let him know he has done the right thing when he sits.

After he begins sitting every time you stand in front of him with a treat in your hand, it is time to add *"Sit"* to the process, saying it just before your Pug begins sitting, then clicking and rewarding as before. Gradually you can phase out the clicker, whose primary value lies in helping your dog to acquire new behaviors.

When Buster has remained in position for five seconds or so, release him by calling him to you. Praise him and give him a treat if you wish, then take up the leash, walk several paces, tell him to sit, and after he does, repeat the *stay* command. Practice this command three or four more times before you end the lesson. As you practice the *stay* command on subsequent days, slowly increase the amount of time Buster stays in place before you release him. Once he begins to master the command, you can practice it indoors. You can practice it while he is standing, too. As the practice sessions continue, you will not need to reinforce the *stay* command by placing your hand in front of his face every time you issue the command.

As Buster learns the *stay* command, you can begin to increase the distance between you and him while he is staying in place. Tell him to stay, set the leash on the ground, and take a small step or two backward. Repeat the *stay* command with the raised-hand signal for reinforcement if Buster looks as if he is about to move. Return him to the sitting position if he does move. After he has stayed in place for 10 or 15 seconds, or however long you want him to remain in place, release him and praise him for being a good dog.

During the course of several training sessions gradually increase the distance between you and Buster to 10 yards (9.1 m). Then, instead of giving the *stay* command and backing away from him, give the command, turn around, walk ten paces, then turn and face him. If he has learned his lessons well, he ought to be sitting obediently in place. If he has followed you instead, repeat the exercise; but this time, after giving the *stay* command, walk only one or two steps before turning and facing him.

GAMES AND GOOD DEEDS

The Pug's cheerfulness and good manners make him a winner in the show ring or on visits to schools, hospitals, and nursing homes.

At a dog show you will find breathtaking dogs on display, vendors who offer the finest in canine accessories, boutiques overflowing with people gifts for you or your dog-loving friends, and a variety of food stands in case all that shopping makes you hungry. The American Kennel Club (AKC) provides a list of dog shows scheduled to be held across the United States (see Information, page 92.) Contact a club near you to ask if there is an admission charge for visitors to the show and to find out how many vendors will be present. Some shows host a few vendors while others roll out a shopping mall.

Dog Shows

When you arrive at a dog show, there will be so much going on that you may feel as if you had walked into a two-hour movie an hour after it had started. Most shows draw at least 1,000 entries, while some attract as many as 2,500 dogs, sometimes more. The majority of those dogs compete in conformation classes for points toward their championships and other awards. Winners are chosen by judges who evaluate each dog according to the written standard for its breed.

Although the AKC recognizes 156 breeds, shows rarely have representatives of every breed in competition. There will be, however, many breeds represented at most shows. Some of the rarer breeds may be represented by only one or two entries, while the more popular breeds may have 30, 40 or even more dogs in competition.

Judging

Judging begins at 8:00 or 8:30 in the morning and lasts until late afternoon. Every dog entered in a show is judged first against other members of his or her breed. In this individual-breed judging, dogs that are not champions are judged first. They are evaluated according to sex; males, which are called "dogs," precede females, which are called "bitches."

Nonchampion dogs or bitches may be entered in one of five classes: puppy, novice, bred by exhibitor, American bred, and open. There are reasons for choosing the class in which to enter a dog, but those reasons need not concern or confuse us here.

After the male classes have been judged, the first-place dogs from each class compete in the winners class. The winner of that class, the winners dog, is awarded points toward his championship. That judging process is then repeated for the bitches in a breed. A dog or a bitch must earn 15 points to become a champion. Those points can be earned one, two, three, four, or five at a time, depending on the number of other entries a dog or a bitch defeats in a particular day's competition.

After the winners bitch has been selected, she, the winners dog, and any champions that have been entered in the show compete in the best-of-breed class. The winner of that class competes later in the day in group judging.

The 156 breeds recognized by the AKC are divided into seven groups—sporting, hound, working, terrier, toy, nonsporting, and herding—according to the purpose for which a breed was created. Pugs compete in the toy group, whose members' primary function is to provide companionship and comic relief. After the seven group winners have been selected,

they return for one more appraisal, the best-in-show competition. The winner from that elite group is the day's top dog.

Obedience Competition

Of all the wonders to be seen at a dog show, the most wondrous occur in the obedience rings, where dogs of various sizes, shapes, and descriptions heed verbal and visual commands as if they (the dogs) were electronically controlled. The handler walks forward; the dog walks at the handler's left side. The handler stops; the dog stops, then sits promptly to await further instruction. The handler tosses an object, the dog remains seated until he is told to move, then retrieves the object and trots back to the handler.

Obedience dogs also jump, lie down, and hold that pose on command. They pick out from a group of objects the one object that a handler has touched, ignoring the objects that do not bear the handler's scent. In one exercise handlers instruct their dogs to lie down, then tell them to stay in that position. The handlers then leave the vicinity for more time than it takes to get a divorce in some states. When the handlers return, their dogs are sitting precisely where they were left.

The Canine Good Citizen Test

The Canine Good Citizen (CGC) test is part of an AKC-sponsored certification program designed to promote canine good manners at home and in the community. CGC tests are administered at a nominal cost, usually $10 or $15, by dog clubs, AKC judges, 4-H leaders,

CHECKLIST

The Makings of a Canine Good Citizen

When your Pug takes the Canine Good Citizen test, you will be required to have with you:
✔ proof of rabies vaccination
✔ a brush or a comb
✔ a buckle or training collar
✔ a six-foot leash

therapy-dog evaluators, veterinarians, vet techs, groomers, private trainers, kennel owners, or by animal control and police K-9 officers. When you are ready to have your dog tested, check with one of those sources or visit the following AKC web page, *akc.org/ events/cgc/cgc_bystate.cfm*, to find an evaluator in your area.

Dogs that successfully complete the CGC test are eligible to receive a Canine Good Citizen certificate from the AKC. With a little help from a friend or two, you can home-school your Pug for the CGC, or you can sign up for CGC classes at a kennel club.

The CGC test comprises 10 individual sections:

1. Accepting a friendly stranger. The evaluator greets the handler in a friendly manner. The dog may not approach the evaluator, nor may he (the dog) act resentful or shy.

2. Sitting politely for petting. The evaluator pets the dog, who is sitting at his handler's side. The dog may stand up as he is being petted, and his handler may talk to him throughout the exercise, but the dog must not exhibit shyness or resentment.

3. Appearance and grooming. Using the handler's comb or brush, the evaluator grooms the dog briefly, examines his ears, and picks up each front foot in turn. The handler may talk to and encourage the dog, who does not have to hold any particular position during this process.

4. Out for a walk. The dog may be on either side of the handler. The evaluator may use a pre-plotted course or may direct the handler verbally. The walk should include a left turn, a right turn, and an about turn, with at least one stop in between and another at the end. The handler may talk to the dog along the way, praise him, or give commands in a normal tone of voice.

5. Walking through a crowd. The dog and handler walk around or close to at least three persons. The dog may show some interest in them, but he should stay with his handler and not display exuberance, shyness, or resentment. The handler may talk to the dog, encouraging him or praising him, throughout the test.

6. *Sit* and *down* on command, and staying in place. The dog's leash is replaced with a 20-foot (6-m) line; then the handler gives the dog the *sit* and *down* commands, touching the dog if necessary to offer guidance. At the evaluator's instruction, the handler tells the dog to stay in either the *sit* or the *down* position, then walks forward the length of the line, turns, and walks back to the dog. The dog must remain where he was left, though he may change position, until the evaluator tells the handler to release the dog.

7. Coming when called. After telling the dog to stay or to wait or giving no command at all the handler walks 10 feet (3 m), turns to face the dog, then calls him, encouraging the dog to come if necessary.

8. Reaction to another dog. Two handlers and their dogs approach each other from a distance of roughly 20 feet (6 m). The handlers stop, shake hands, exchange pleasantries, then continue on for about 10 feet (3 m). The dogs should show no more than casual interest in each other.

9. Reaction to distraction. The evaluator presents two distractions—dropping a chair, a crutch, or a cane, rolling a crate dolly past the dog, or having a jogger run in front of the dog. The dog may express some interest and curiosity and may even appear startled, but he should not panic, try to run away, show aggressiveness, or bark. The handler may talk to the dog and encourage or praise him during the exercise.

10. Supervised separation. The handler gives the dog's lead to the evaluator and walks out of sight of the dog, who is expected to remain with the evaluator for three minutes. The dog does not have to stay in one position, but he should not bark, whine, or pace continually, or show anything stronger than mild agitation or nervousness. The evaluator may talk to the dog but should not engage in excessive talking or petting.

T I P

Tips for First-time Rally Exhibitors
✔ Register your Pug with the AKC.
✔ Visit the AKC website (*akc.org/events/ rally/index.cfm*) to find a rally-training club.
✔ Attend training classes with your dog.
✔ Become familiar with AKC rally regulations.
✔ Attend a rally to observe ring procedures.
✔ Make sure your Pug's inoculations are current.

Rally

The rally is more rigorous than the CGC test, but less formal than obedience competition and less physically demanding than agility trials, for which Pugs as a tribe are not so well suited as are some of the more athletic breeds. AKC rally trials are open to all dogs at least six months of age who are registered with the AKC or listed with the AKC Purebred Alternative Listing/Indefinite Listing Privilege or recorded with the Foundation Stock Service.

Although Pugs are not known as agility dogs, this one seems to have mastered the ins and outs of one agility test.

In rally competition dog-and-handler teams complete a predetermined course comprising 10 to 20 stations. The exact number depends on the level of the competition—rally novice, rally advanced, or rally excellent. Each station is marked with a sign that provides instructions regarding the command to be executed there. These commands may require a dog to sit or to lie down as his handler walks once around him; to turn with his handler 270 or 360 degrees to the right or to the left; to walk at a fast or a slow pace to the next station; to halt, stand briefly, and then lie down; to back up three steps from a halt; to jump a barrier; to weave between pylons, etc.

Before competition begins, handlers may walk the course without their dogs in order to familiarize themselves with its requirements. A copy of the course is posted at ringside so that exhibitors know what to expect and where to go once they are in the ring.

At the *forward* command from the judge, a dog-and-handler team sets off on the course. The dog must be under the control of the

Choosing a Trainer for Your Pug

You do not need a Ph.D. to train your Pug entirely at home, but unless you plan to keep your Pug entirely at home, you will want him to obey commands when there are other dogs and people around. Obedience classes provide the company of other dogs and people, and chances are you and your Pug will benefit from and enjoy attending classes conducted by a reputable and competent dog trainer.

Leads to dog trainers can be found through the Yellow Pages, the Internet, veterinarians' offices, humane societies, boarding kennels, or dog groomers; but selecting the first trainer you find is like choosing a restaurant without reading more than one review. In selecting a dog trainer a "review" means visiting the trainer's home or training location to ask a few questions and to see how his or her dogs behave. At the very least you will want to know the following about a prospective trainer for your Pug:

✔ How long has the trainer been training?
✔ Is the trainer qualified as an evaluator for the Canine Good Citizen Program?
✔ Does the trainer hold current membership in any dog training or behavior associations?
✔ Does the trainer provide written handouts?
✔ What correction methods does the trainer use?
✔ Does the trainer permit treats as training aids?
✔ How large are the classes?
✔ Do people and dogs receive some individual attention?
✔ Are all dogs required to have proof of vaccination before starting a class?

handler at his or her left side as they go. Each performance is timed, but times count only in case of a tie.

Handlers are permitted unlimited communication with their dogs, including talk, praise, encouragement, hand claps, leg slaps, etc. A handler may not touch his dog, however, nor may the handler use loud or harsh commands or intimidating signals.

Therapy Work

Pugs are naturals at therapy work. Therapy dogs and their owners visit hospitals or nursing homes, bringing warmth and companionship to the residents. In addition to being petted and fussed over, therapy dogs may interact with a patient by retrieving a toy thrown by that patient.

Therapy dogs visit schools, too, where they serve as attentive, nonjudgmental listeners while children read to them. Because Pugs are so reliable with children, they are excellent candidates for this job.

Before you and your Pug set out for the nearest school or nursing home, contact the Delta Society (425.679.5500 or *deltasociety.org*) or Therapy Dogs International (973.252.9800 or *tdi-dog.org*) to find out how your Pug can become a registered therapy dog by passing a test similar to the Canine Good Citizen test.

The therapy-dog test includes exercises in which a dog interacts with a person in a wheelchair, on crutches, or using a walker.

Your Pug does not need a certificate in order to serve as a therapy dog, but his chances of being accepted, and the chances of his therapy visits going more smoothly, are enhanced by formal training.

Informal Obedience Training

What if dog shows had obedience trials that included exercises like "stop chewing that at once" or "don't bark every time the doorbell rings"—practical, everyday stuff like that? After all, how many times will there be 10 wallets lying in a pile on the living room floor and you will want your Pug to go over and pick out yours? Why not drag a sofa into a show ring instead, lead a Pug in, and as soon as he begins chewing on it, give his owner 15 seconds to get him to stop? The owner who accomplishes that feat in the fewest seconds is the winner and gets to keep the sofa.

Until the AKC wakes up to the need for informal obedience training, Pug owners will have to fill in the gaps by spending lots of time with their dogs, socializing and training them properly, and correcting behavior problems before they occur. The following tips will aid in those regards:

✔ Do not ignore undesirable behavior; it will not go away on its own. Do something about it when it happens.

✔ Distract your Pug immediately when he misbehaves; he has at best a 10-second attention span, so give him a chew bone that tastes better than a chair leg.

✔ In a pinch, resort to formal commands like *Sit* and *Stay* when the doorbell rings and your Pug begins to race toward the door with every intention of hurling himself against it. What do you have to lose except your patience?

TIP

The Last Words

Training a Pug is not so difficult as herding cats, nor is it so easy as operating a sheep dog by remote control. Somewhere between those extremes lies the promised land, a land that you can reach, we promise, if you keep your wits about you and help your Pug to keep his wits about him too.

THE ELDERLY PUG

Inside every young Pug there is an old Pug waiting to get out.

Your Pug dog may be getting old if he mistakes your leg for his favorite tree, if he does not hear you calling unless you are looking at him, if his get-up-and-go seems to have gotten up and went, or if he sleeps as if he is in hibernation.

All Pugs do not age in the same fashion or at the same rate, nor do all systems in any single Pug age in unison. An aging Pug may still hear the sound of kibble clanging into his bowl, but he may not find his way to the kitchen as quickly as he did in the past. Yet, no matter how fast or slowly your Pug ages, you can soften some of the effects of the aging process by providing him with good, proactive veterinary care, an age-appropriate diet, and the extra loving attention his situation requires.

Hear's the Thing

Barring accident or severe illness, a Pug does not lose his hearing overnight. It declines over many nights and days, though you may not have noticed because your Pug compensated for his hearing loss by relying more on his other senses. He still may bark when you return home, for example, but he is barking because he picked up your scent, not because he heard the door open.

You should not assume that your Pug's ability to compensate for his diminished hearing guarantees that its cause is age related. Have your Pug examined by his veterinarian to determine if there is an underlying medical reason for your Pug's hearing loss.

Coping with Hearing Loss

You should be as clever as your Pug is about adjusting to his diminished hearing. Avoid

▬▬►PUG FACT▬▬

Because a Pug's life expectancy is roughly 12 to 15 years, he reaches old age somewhere between his ninth and twelfth birthdays.

startling him, especially while he is sleeping or eating. Alert him to your presence by clapping your hands, whistling shrilly, or positioning yourself so that he can see you.

If your Pug responds to any of these cues, employ them consistently, and praise him when he responds to them. Praise him also for making eye contact with you, as this will encourage him to look to you for cues more often.

Dogs who hear less bark more, simply to feel the vibrations in their throats or to "hear" themselves. This barking can be annoying for owners whose dogs have not been barkers before.

Do You Hear What I Hear?

Always keep a hearing-challenged Pug on a lead when he is away from the safety of his fenced-in yard. He may not hear cars or other dogs approaching, so he depends on you to keep him out of harm's way and to keep harm's way out of his.

As Lights Grow Dim

The loss of vision—because it is most often incremental—does not prevent a Pug from getting around in familiar territory. Indeed, you may not notice your Pug's loss of vision unless you rearrange the furniture one day and he walks into chairs that turn up in unfamiliar places.

As long as the food bowl, the water dish, and his favorite chair remain where he expects

TIP

Landmarks

You can help your Pug "see" his way around by using scents to mark areas in your house. Use a scent like lemon oil or potpourri to mark areas such as stair landings. If your Pug has difficulty locating his water bowl, put a drop of vanilla extract on the mat beneath the bowl or, better yet, add a splash of flavored dog water to his bowl when you freshen it each day.

Another scent to which a Pug responds favorably is his own. Do not wash his toys unless they begin to glow in the dark. Ditto for his bedding.

them to be, even a legally blind Pug can get around nicely. He also can manage walks along his favorite routes if you keep him on a lead and give him time to sniff his way on familiar paths.

Weight Control

Older Pugs often gain weight even though we feed them no more than usual. This happens because their metabolic rates slow down and their muscles begin to waste. Sometimes an aging Pug's tendency to gain weight can be off-set by reducing the amount you are feeding him or by feeding him a lite or a senior dog food: one that contains fewer calories, less protein, less fat, and more fiber than regular food does.

Troublesome Weight Issues

Like other signs of aging, weight gain may have sinister implications. If weight gain is caused by the accumulation of fluid in the abdominal cavity, a condition known as ascites, heart failure is probably the cause. An elderly Pug that begins to look pregnant, and is afflicted by shortness of breath, coughing, or difficult breathing, should be examined by a veterinarian.

Cushing's syndrome and Cushing's disease are additional causes of weight gain in elderly Pugs. Cushing's syndrome is caused by a tumor of the adrenal gland, while Cushing's disease, which occurs much more frequently than Cushing's syndrome, is caused by a tumor on the pituitary gland. Both tumors that lead to Cushing's are usually benign.

Among the symptoms of Cushing's are increased or excessive drinking, urination, or appetite, an enlarged, distended abdomen, and

obesity. If a Pug exhibits any of these symptoms, and is lethargic, short of breath, and/or less inclined to interact with his owners, he should be examined by a veterinarian.

Like weight gain, progressive weight loss in older dogs is cause for concern, perhaps even more so. Weight loss may be an indication of kidney failure, the presence of a tumor, diabetes mellitus, liver disease, or other conditions. If your dog loses weight for two or three consecutive weeks, schedule an appointment with your veterinarian.

Exercise Needs

An elderly Pug's activities may be limited by arthritis and muscle atrophy, but you can help him to maintain muscle tone and suppleness, to increase blood circulation, and to improve gastrointestinal motility (the spontaneous movement of the gut) by encouraging him to take part in moderate exercise, such as a leisurely walk, each day. If his daily walk consists of three turns around the block, reduce that number to one or two, or replace one extended walk with two or three short walks.

Symptoms of Diseases

Although research does not indicate that elderly Pugs are more susceptible to kidney disease, diabetes mellitus, or liver disease than other elderly dogs are, you should be aware of the symptoms of those conditions.

	Kidney Disease	Diabetes Mellitus	Liver Disease
Abnormally colored gums		x	
Appetite changes	x	x	x
Behavioral changes	x		x
Change in activity level	x		
Diarrhea	x		x
Increased thirst or urination	x	x	x
Seizures	x		x
Urinary incontinence	x		
Vomiting	x	x	x
Weakness/exercise intolerance	x		
Weight loss	x	x	x

Pay close attention to your Pug at the conclusion of a walk or a round of play. If he seems stressed or if he tires more quickly than he used to do, it is probably time to cut back on his minutes. Be especially attentive to labored breathing or to the sudden onset of fatigue as these may be signs of heart disease.

Grooming an Older Pug

If you have been grooming your Pug two or three times a week, continue that routine and continue to examine him for external parasites, skin rashes, bald spots, lumps, and lesions.

The discovery of suspicious lumps or lesions, of course, warrants an immediate call to your veterinarian. Persistent rashes and spreading bald spots will need professional attention also.

Some days your Pug may not be so receptive to grooming as he usually is. He may fuss and squirm as he did when he was a puppy. Indeed, elderly Pugs can act much like puppies in grooming and in other ways. Rather than making a federal case out of grooming sessions, make them shorter and more frequent than usual in order to accommodate your Pug's shortened attention span.

Fighting Teeth and Nails

You ignore your Pug's teeth at his and your peril. When teeth are ignored, tartar accumulates; and when it does, gingivitis and weakened tooth structure are sure to follow, making eating a chore at a time when a Pug's appetite may be on the decline for other reasons, and making your Pug more prone to secondary infections that could become life threatening.

If you have neglected your Pug's teeth, and if he is willing to learn new tricks, review the information about dental care on pages 53–55

and begin brushing his teeth several times a week. If he does not like this idea, at least have his teeth cleaned and scaled by your veterinarian at semiannual checkups.

Pugs are scarcely more happy about having their nails cut than they are about having their teeth cleaned. Granted, an overgrown toenail does not have the same potential for harm as gingivitis does, but overgrown nails are a source of discomfort nevertheless, and no dog, particularly an aging one, needs another thorn in that crown.

Personality Changes in the Elderly Pug

The older Pugs get, the less adaptable they are to changes in their daily routines. Those

TIP

Semiannual Is the New Annual

Because an older Pug is more susceptible to disease and less able to defeat it, an annual checkup is no longer sufficient to monitor his health. From roughly the age of nine, or sooner if your veterinarian suggests, your Pug's annual checkup ought to become semiannual, and it ought to include a chemical blood screen test on each visit. With an older Pug you want the bad news first and you want it early if you hope to give your Pug the best chance of warding off or at least controlling a problem.

changes include, but are not limited to, being sent to a boarding kennel, moving to a new house, or welcoming another pet into the family.

You may not be able to refuse a promotion that involves moving halfway across the country, but vacation choices and new pet acquisitions are matters you can control. Put off the trip to Bermuda, and vacation someplace close to home, someplace that welcomes dogs.

Housetraining Revisited

An elderly Pug may have to go outside more often than the three or four times a day to which he is accustomed. If lessened bladder control spills over into incontinence while your Pug is sleeping, the cause may be weakening muscles. Your veterinarian can prescribe medications to put a clamp on, or at least to dial down, this problem.

Incontinence may spring from a low-grade bladder infection. Dogs are susceptible to bladder infections because the opening to the canine bladder is more lax than it is in humans. As a consequence, bacteria have an easier time gaining access to a dog's bladder and doing mischief there.

Bladder infections can be treated with antibiotics, but if that treatment is not effective, your veterinarian may want to run a blood test or to take X-rays to check for the presence of a tumor.

Another source of incontinence in older dogs is the onset of kidney failure. As dogs

TIP

Coping with Incontinence

While your Pug is being treated for incontinence, there are several things you can do to make him more comfortable.

✔ Protect his mattress—or yours if he is still sleeping on it—with a plastic cover or shower curtain.

✔ Protect your Pug by draping a layer of fleece, which does not retain liquid, on top of his bed.

✔ Wash his bedding as often as necessary to keep it sanitary.

age, blood flow to the kidneys decreases, and they are less able to regulate the concentration of water as well as soluble substances such as sodium salts by filtering the blood, reabsorbing what is needed, and excreting the rest as urine. As a result, the kidneys fail to concentrate urine effectively, so older dogs with deteriorating kidney function have to drink and to urinate more often. To help prevent kidney failure, make sure your Pug has access to water at all times and feed him a diet that contains a low amount of high-quality protein, if your veterinarian recommends it.

Spay Incontinence

The most common cause of urinary incontinence in dogs is spay incontinence. Also known as estrogen-responsive incontinence or hormonally responsive incontinence, this condition can occur in spayed females at any time, from immediately after spaying to several years

later. If your Pug is diagnosed with spay incontinence, your veterinarian can recommend an appropriate treatment.

Saying Good-bye

Time eventually asserts its claim on all Pugs. They become so measured in their movements, so determined in their sleep that they take on the aspect of ghost dogs: their bodies are present, but their spirits are preparing to take their leaves.

When your Pug reaches this stage, you may have to decide between prolonging or ending his life. That is a decision in which selfishness cannot play a part.

No matter how much you want to sustain your relationship with your Pug, if your veterinarian tells you that your dog is in pain and that the quality of his life is substandard, you owe it to your dog to end that suffering.

If your veterinarian is willing to come to your house to euthanize your Pug, arrange for that service so your Pug's final moments will be spent in familiar surroundings. If your veterinarian does not make house calls, he or she may be willing to euthanize your Pug in your car. This can be a comfort for dogs who are upset by the tension in a veterinarian's office.

If you must take your Pug to the veterinarian's office to be euthanized, arrange to wait in the car until the veterinarian can attend to your Pug. Do not simply hand your dog over to an attendant and take a seat in the waiting room. Your Pug was always there when you needed him—and more than a few times when you did not. You owe it to him to be the last person who holds him when it is time to leave this world.

INFORMATION

National Breed Club

The Pug Dog Club of America
www.pugs.org
Donna Manha, Secretary
449 Maar Avenue
Fremont, CA 94536
E-mail: *pugsrus2@comcast.net*

Canine Registries

American Canine Association, Inc.
P.O. Box 808
Phoenixville, PA 19460
800.651.8332
800.422.1864 (Fax)
www.acacanines.com

American Kennel Club
Customer Care
8051 Arco Corporate Drive, Suite 100
Raleigh, NC 27617-3390
919.233.9767
8:30 A.M.–5:00 P.M. ET
www.akc.org

The Canadian Kennel Club
200 Ronson Drive, Suite 400
Etobicoke, Ontario
M9W 5Z9
416.675.5511
www.ckc.ca/en/

United Kennel Club
100 East Kilgore Road
Kalamazoo, MI 49002-5584
269.343.9020
www.ukcdogs.com

On-line Resources

PugsCom   *www.pugs.com*
PugCenter   *www.pugcenter.com*
Pugs.nl   *www.pugs.nl*

Health, Welfare, and Medical Organizations

American Animal Hospital Association
12575 W. Bayaud Avenue
Lakewood, CO 80228
303.986.2800
303.986.1700 (Fax)
E-mail: *info@aahanet.org*
www.aahanet.org

American Kennel Club Canine Health
 Foundation
251 W. Garfield Road
Aurora, OH 44202
216.995.0806
E-mail: *akchf@aol.com*

American Society for the Prevention
 of Cruelty to Animals
424 East 92nd Street
New York, NY 10128-6804
212.876.7700 (General number)
800.628.0028 (Donations & membership)
www.aspca.org

American Veterinary Medical Association
1931 North Meacham Road, Suite 100
Schaumburg, IL 60173-4360
800.248.2862
847.925.1329 (Fax)
www.avma.org

Canine Eye Registration Foundation
VMDB/CERF
Lynn Hall
625 Harrison Street
Purdue University
W. Lafayette, IN 47907-2026
E-mail: *CERF@vmdb.org*
www.vmdb.org/cerf.html

Delta Society
875 124th Avenue NE
Suite 101
Bellevue, WA 98005
425.679.5500
425.679.5539 (Fax)
8:30 A.M.–4:30 P.M. Monday-Friday, PST
www.deltasociety.org

The Humane Society of the United States
2100 L Street, NW
Washington, D.C. 20037
Attn: Member Services
202.452.1100
E-mail: *humanesociety@humanesociety.org*

ASPCA Animal Poison Control Center
Dana B. Farbman, CVT
Senior Manager, Client and Professional
    Relations
1717 South Philo Road, Suite #36
Urbana, IL 61802
217.337.5030
217.344.3586 (Fax)
E-mail: *dfarbman@apcc.aspca.org*

Orthopedic Foundation for Animals
2300 E. Nifong Boulevard
Columbia, MO 65201-3806
573.442.0418
E-mail: *ofa@offa.org*
8:00 A.M. to 4:30 P.M. CST

Lost Pet Registries

AVID ID Systems, Inc.
3185 Hamner Avenue
Norco, CA 92860-1983
800.336.AVID (2843)
951.737.8967 (Fax)
E-mail: avid@AvidID.com
www.AvidID.com

Home Again Microchip Service
888.466.3242
E-mail: *customerservice@homeagain.com*
www.homeagainpets.com

National Dog Registry
P.O. Box 118
Woodstock, NY 12498-0116
800.637.3647
www.nationaldogregistry.com

Petfinders
368 High Street
Athol, NY 12810
800.223.4747
www.petfinder.com

The American Kennel Club
AKC Companion Recovery
5580 Centerview Drive, Suite 250
Raleigh, NC 27606-3394
800.252.7894
E-mail: *found@akc.org*
www.akc.org/car.htm

Bibliography

Belmonte, Brenda. *The Pug Handbook.*
    Hauppauge, NY: Barron's Educational Series,
    2005.
Gewirtz, Elaine Waldorf. *Pugs for Dummies.*
    Hoboken, NJ: For Dummies, 2004.
Kaufman, Margo. *Clara: The Story of the Pug
    Who Ruled My Life.* New York, NY: Plume,
    1999.
Maggitti, Phil. *Postcards from the Pug Bus.*
    Irvine, CA: Doral Publishing, 2004.
Palika, Liz. *The Complete Idiot's Guide to Pugs.*
    New York, NY: Alpha, 2005.
Rice, Dan, D.V.M. *Pugs* (Barron's Dog Bibles).
    Hauppauge, NY: Barron's Educational Series,
    2009.

I N D E X

About the Author

Phil Maggitti is a freelance writer and editor living happily ever after in southeastern Pennsylvania with his wife Mary Ann, eight Pug dogs and seven cats. Mr. Maggitti has received a number of awards for his writing, including two awards from the American Horse Council—for best feature article in 1985 and for best personal column in 1986—and one award from Dog Writers Association of America for best single-breed booklet in 1994.

Other Barron's titles by Phil Maggitti:
Birman Cats: A Complete Pet Owner's Manual (1996)
Before You Buy That Kitten (1995)
Guide to a Well-Behaved Cat (1993)
Scottish Fold Cats: A Complete Pet Owner's Manual (1993)

Photo Credits

Norvia Behling: pages 34, 40, 42, 57; Seth Casteel: pages 4, 5, 6, 7 (top), 8, 12, 15, 16, 18, 22, 27, 29, 46, 47, 49, 54, 60, 62, 64, 65, 66, 68, 69, 71; Tara Darling: pages 9 (top, bottom); Jean Fogle: pages 7 (bottom), 10, 19, 20, 23, 25, 33, 37, 39, 45, 84, 86, 89, 90; Isabelle Francais: pages 11, 35, 36; Daniel Johnson: page 30; Paulette Johnson: pages 32, 38, 43, 59; Shutterstock: pages 79, 81; Kira Stackhouse: pages 2–3, 13, 31, 48, 51, 52, 61, 73, 76, 77, 85; Connie Summers/Paulette Johnson: page 74, 83.

Important Note

This book is concerned with selecting, keeping, and raising Pugs. The publisher and the author think it is important to point out that the advice and information for Pug maintenance applies to healthy, normally developed animals. Anyone who acquires an adult dog or one from an animal shelter must consider that the animal may have behavioral problems and may, for example, bite without any visible provocation. Such anxiety bites are dangerous for the owner as well as the general public.

Caution is further advised in the association of children with dogs, in meetings with other dogs, and in exercising the dog without a leash.

Cover Photos

Shutterstock: front cover, back cover, inside front cover, inside back cover.

A Note About Pronouns

Many dog lovers feel that the pronoun "it" is not appropriate when referring to a pet that can be such a wonderful part of our lives. For this reason, Pugs are described as "he" throughout this book unless the topic specifically relates to female dogs. This by no means infers any preference, nor should it be taken as an indication that either sex is particularly problematic.

All inquiries should be addressed to:
Barron's Educational Series, Inc.
250 Wireless Boulevard
Hauppauge, NY 11788
www.barronseduc.com

Library of Congress Catalog Card No. 2010016922

ISBN-13: 978-0-7641-4325-0
ISBN-10: 0-7641-4325-5

Library of Congress Cataloging-in-Publication Data
Maggitti, Phil.
    Pugs / Phil Maggitti.
        p. cm. — (A complete pet owner's manual)
    Includes bibliographical references and index.
    ISBN-13: 978-0-7641-4325-0 (alk. paper)
    ISBN-10: 0-7641-4325-5 (alk. paper)
  1. Pug. I. Title.
  SF429.P9M34 2010
  636.76—dc22   2010016922

Printed in China

9 8 7 6 5 4 3 2 1